I am Uluru

A FAMILY'S STORY

BY JEN COWLEY
WITH THE ULURU FAMILY

Published in October, 2018 as a project facilitated by not-for-profit organisation Kungka Kutjara Aboriginal Corporation in conjunction with and on behalf of the Uluru family.
All proceeds from this project will be returned to community to help preserve and maintain Anangu culture and language.

Funded by the Commonwealth Department of Communications and The Arts.

Words by Jen Cowley (www.jencowley.com) with **language interpreting/translations by** Kathy Tozer and as told by members of the Uluru family.
Project co-ordinator Mark Horton
Cover photo by Steve Cowley
Images by Jen Cowley, Steve Cowley, and as acknowledged. All images are subject to copyright.
Graphic Design by Sarah Head Creative (www.sarahhead.com.au)
Printed by Omne (www.omne.com.au)

ISBN: 978-0-6484120-0-7

Australian Government

Indigenous Languages and Arts

I am Uluru

A FAMILY'S STORY

BY JEN COWLEY
WITH THE ULURU FAMILY

It is customary in many indigenous communities, and in Anangu culture, that the names of the deceased not be mentioned and their images not be reproduced until such time as the family deems it appropriate.
Anangu, and all people of Aboriginal and Torres Strait Island descent, are advised that this publication contains the names and images of some people who have died.

contents

FOREWORD

Ulurulanguru Alice Springs-alakutu ankula kulilkatiningina book pala palunya. Nyangatja tjinguru tjukurpa pulka mulapa, Anangu tjuta kulira nintiringkuntjaku. Anangu maru tjuta kulintjaku. Anangu tjutaku Tjukurpa kulintjaku. Ara irititja tjuta kulintjaku. Paper palatja tjukurpa wiru, read-amilara kulini, tjinguru kulilku, tjituru-tjituru nganampa yaaltji yaaltji mala ngaraku?

Mutitjululanguru ankula kulira kulira kulilkatiningi, mununa tjituru-tjituru. Ngarakatinguna ilany pakara. Palula tjituru-tjituru ngarangi panya, ilanypa pakanyangka.

Uti nyarangku kulintjaku. Walka tjunkuntjaku ngaranyi. Tjungungku nyinara palyantjaku. Wiyangka, wall purunypa ngaranyi ngururpa. Ngapartji ngapartji nyuntu nganananya putu kulini nganana ngapartji putu kulini.

I was driving from Uluru to Alice Springs and I was thinking about this book, thinking it might be a really big story for people to learn about and understand. And that Anangu themselves need to know; to understand their own history. These pages hold valuable stories. If they're read, maybe people will think about our heartbreak and what the future holds for us.

Driving from Mutitjulu I was thinking and thinking all the way and it made me so sad. You know I had to pull over because I started to cry. I stood there with tears streaming down my cheeks.

People out there need to understand. We need to write it all down. Then we can work together. Otherwise, we can't understand each other – it's like there's a giant wall between us. I can't come across and you can't come across.

Sammy Wilson (Tjama Uluru) 2018

PREFACE
—

There's a certain colour that's unique to the red centre of Australia; a particular shade of purplish pink that paints the landscape for just a few tantalising minutes as the sun sets over the central desert. It's a blush that comes in those few precious seconds after the day's grand finale – a blazing, fiery sunset that makes Uluru look like a chunk of heaven that's fallen from the sun itself.

You can't see this astonishing veil of colour by looking directly at it. It disappears under direct gaze. You have to look to the side, avert your eyes, use your peripheral vision, to see it properly. Those lucky enough to be able to glimpse it will witness for those few minutes the true essence, the heart, of the red centre's palette.

So it is with Tjukurpa – the ancient Anangu faith – and the same is true of the Uluru family's story. Look directly at it and you won't see its majesty.

Not until you squint the eye of your consciousness can you take in the entire view and see it not as a seemingly disjointed collection of tales and thoughts and experiences and recollections, but as a whole beautiful picture. The Uluru family story is like a hand-made quilt with the individual pieces all a different shade, a different texture, a different size. Not until it is stitched together does its collective beauty and meaning become clear. And this is just a small part of a much larger quilt.

When I was invited by members of the Uluru family to help tell their story, I was still far from the point of comprehending the necessity of using peripheral vision to take in the entire view. They knew this. I didn't. But they also knew that, with their guidance, I would come to understand the nuances and intricacies of the Anangu way and the retelling of the story would be richer for that learning. It is only with hindsight that I can fully appreciate the enormity of both their trust and the privilege afforded by that initial invitation.

The Uluru family's motivation for undertaking to tell their story is twofold. With the passage of time and the subsequently inevitable erosion of traditional ways, the recording of stories and recollections is a race against the generational clock. The family's elders fear the loss of their knowledge and history, and their fervent wish is to preserve – in the modern way of the written word – as much as they can before it is forever lost to coming generations.

But the family also acknowledges a well-intentioned thirst for understanding from the wider, non-Anangu world. The Anangu way is to share and the Uluru family accepts that inviting visitors into their world is also a way to help preserve their precious culture and knowledge, just as they have accepted the need to embrace the contemporary world in which they now live.

Their hope is that through fostering a greater understanding of their culture, others will help with its preservation and so the Uluru family has chosen, for the first time in a forum such as this, to open up as much of their traditional world as is possible so that others might come to understand why certain elements of Anangu culture must remain secret and sacred if they are to remain safe.

Inherent in this cultural landscape are challenges that make the conventional account of a family's story an impossibility.

It is important, if the family's aim of nurturing a deeper understanding of their story is to be achieved, that some of these challenges be explained ahead of a dive into its pages. While the contextual narrative that underscores the retelling of the stories will help, there are some things the reader will need to know about the parts to fully appreciate the whole.

The recollections and information on which this story is based came largely from elders for whom English is often a third, fourth or even fifth tongue, so while the translations were as accurate as possible there are certain nuances of language that have required some tweaking. Like most indigenous Australian languages, the Anangu word was not written until only very recent times. Many Anangu are able to listen to and understand English far more clearly than they are able to speak it.

For a story such as this, the eliciting of feelings and emotions are integral, however it is difficult to accurately or appropriately translate the word "feeling". There is a word, "kulini", that encompasses a number of perspectives – it means to listen, hear, think about/consider, decide, know about, understand, remember, have a premonition from a sensation in the body, and yes, to feel. Ask directly "How did you feel?" and Anangu will wonder which of these perspectives to draw on. Thanks to the close proximity to which Anangu live with each other in community, they are so finely tuned to the feelings of others they rarely need to ask the question. Some imagination and gentle creativity have therefore been necessary to fill in those emotional gaps.

Hindsight is also not part of the Anangu way, so asking for reflections is difficult, as is eliciting recollections of what Uluru family members were thinking at a particular time. Westerners tend to analyse everything; culturally we are looking for the "whys" and looking for answers. Anangu preoccupations are different. They live in the present.

With this in mind, it is ineffective to approach a project such as this using a conventional chronological framework. Dates, times and deadlines have little relevance for Anangu. For instance, there is no direct translation in their languages for the word "day" – the best we could approximate was "sun's up" – so piecing together a family timeline has been tricky, as has the unique and complex Anangu system of kinship and family. This may at times make the story seem disjointed to those who are used to conventional historical accounts, but dates and times are not the essence of this story.

It is similarly not the Anangu culture to learn by asking questions, nor to teach by responding to direct questions. The elders set the pace of learning and in doing so, teach the fundamental art of listening. Our conditioning makes questioning a widely accepted process but for Anangu, it can be experienced as mildly offensive in the sense that it can feel like a challenge to their way of teaching and to their knowledge itself. Prolonged and repeated questioning, therefore, becomes something of a visceral invasion. It's about respecting boundaries and it was important throughout this process to allow the Uluru family tell their stories in their way.

The passing on of knowledge comes not chronologically but at a time and a pace the elders believe is appropriate.

While this was initially frustrating for a journalist (particularly of the female variety) whose default setting is to fire direct questions based on the "who, what, when, where, why" approach, the beauty and effectiveness of their way soon became clear. They knew far better than I what I needed to know, but more importantly, when I needed and was ready to know it. They taught me when I was ready to learn and as a result the knowledge and stories gathered have far deeper meaning. I was then able to stitch together what had for so long felt like a mish-mash of disjointed patchwork pieces.

I am neither anthropologist nor sociologist, linguist nor demographer. Neither am I a conventional historian.

I am a storyteller for the Uluru family.

And this is their story.

—

Jen Cowley, October 2018

TJUKURPA

—

Tjukurpa panya tjamulu, kamilu, mamalu, ngunytjulu nganananya ungu, kurunpangka munu katangka kanyintjaku – (Pitjantjatjara language)

This Law was given to us by our grandfathers and grandmothers, our fathers and mothers, to hold onto in our heads and in our hearts.[1]

Tjukurpa (pronounced jook-oor-pa) is the Anangu faith – the foundation for life and society and describes the Anangu ancestral connection to the land, their culture and to others. For Anangu, and for the Uluru family, Tjukurpa is everything. It binds them to each other and to the land. It guides them throughout their lives, enshrines the creation and ancestral stories and decrees the law. It defines the Anangu way of thinking and living.

To apply a comparison with other faiths, under Tjukurpa the land itself is the sacred scripture. Every rock, every tree, every animal and plant and natural feature is part of that scripture. The land is all sacred under Tjukurpa, but certain sites and animals, for instance, are sacrosanct to individuals, families or groups according to kinship, birthplace, gender or story-line.

Tjukurpa refers to the creation period when the ancestral beings, Tjukuritja, created the world as it is now known, and from this came the religion, law and moral structure that form the basis of Anangu society. The words "dreamtime" or "dreaming" have become part of the wider vernacular to conveniently describe indigenous Australian society and history, and although some Anangu themselves now use the term for ease of translation, in general they reject that Tjukurpa is a dream. There is no word in the languages for "dreamtime". For Anangu and the Uluru

---

1. Uluru Kata-Tjuta National Park fact sheet; Parks Australia, 2015

family, Tjukurpa is truth.

Daily life is guided by the tenets and learnings of Tjukurpa, which is like a sophisticated code, with knowledge handed down through ceremony, song, dance and art. Tjukurpa teaches the right way and warns of the dangers of the wrong way. It ensures survival. It sets down traditional law as well as the right way of imposing penalties for breaking that law.

As with language, Tjukurpa is memorised rather than written like, say, the bible. Anangu are culturally obliged to hand the knowledge down to the right people, usually along family and gender lines. Ceremonies play a significant role in this teaching, as does spending time "on country" with elders who possess the knowledge. Certain people have certain responsibilities in maintaining different parts of Tjukurpa, which may relate to a particular site or story or song-line, and it is vital that it be correctly passed on to those who have inherited the right to the knowledge.

Knowledge from Tjukurpa is the Anangu inheritance. Just as anyone would guard such a significant legacy, so too do Anangu protect theirs. It is this legacy they are shielding when they explain, as the Uluru family hopes to do with this story, why there is much they can share with non-Anangu people, but much again that must stay with its rightful owners as Tjukurpa demands.

FAMILY AND KINSHIP

Understanding the way in which Anangu kinship structures work can be a mind-numbingly complex exercise for those used to the conventional, western idea of family based largely on blood ties.

Anangu family ties are intricate and based on a sophisticated system of kinship that recognises biological bonds only as a small part of a much more intricate structure. Kinship can also be forged through ceremony and through country and language. Tjukurpa outlines relationships and sets down the proper way of connecting with others, including through marriage and other ties between men and women of all ages. Obligation and responsibility to family extends to the entire language group, which can further complicate the process of applying a whitefella approach to understanding Anangu kinship. For Anangu, the "where" is just as important as the "who", with family groups and ties largely determined by country.

While there are similarities with non-Anangu family ties, for Anangu all your father's brothers are your fathers and your mother's sisters are your mothers. All those we would call cousins are brothers and sisters – there is no traditional word for cousin. All uncles and brothers in a family are fathers to all the children who follow. This is particularly important when it comes to inheritance of knowledge, which traditionally goes from grandparent to grandchild, rather than from parent to child.

In the way of Anangu kinship, people can be of the same age but referred to as aunties and uncles and grandparents in the same way that one will often meet Anangu who are many years apart in age but are brothers and sisters because of kinship.

Inherent within this sophisticated kinship structure is the

imperative of ensuring not only the survival of family knowledge lines and connection to country but of maintaining a strong genetic mix by determining "right way-wrong way" for marriage.

Anangu also have a quite delightful and deeply significant process of what non-Anangu would call adoption. Anangu call it nyuyuntja. It is not the paperwork and officialdom style of adoption, but refers to the forging of bonds through helping to raise someone. Anangu, including members of the Uluru family as will become apparent, often say "he/she grew me up" or "I grew him/her up" and so refer to that person as either a parent or their child. "Growing someone up" is perfectly normal and widely practiced in Anangu society and is a source of great pride, deep affection and lifelong bonds. Nyuyuntja also means that no Anangu child is ever an orphan.

Myriad resources exist for the curious reader to further explore the fascinating and complex nuances of Anangu kinship and family structures, but for the purposes of the telling of the Uluru family story, it is enough to simply acknowledge and accept the Anangu world view when it comes to defining family. After all, it's been around for a very, very long time.

I AM Uluru

August, 2016

At precisely twelve noon on a day when the mercury has already shot well past the forecast high of 32 degrees, a gleaming white tour bus hisses to a halt outside the pristine glass-fronted reception of a Yulara hotel.

It regurgitates a stream of chattering tourists who alternately swat away flies and sweat as they emerge from the cool of the coach to make a dash across the hot-plate of pavement for the air-conditioned comfort of the lobby.

Cameras slung 'round necks, selfie sticks aloft, fly nets secured to vented hats, sensible walking shoes peeking out from beneath khaki cargo pants, backpacks dangling from shoulders. Despite the eclectic mix of nationalities and ages, there's a certain sameness to the wave after wave of visitors to this central Australian resort town.

They have come from every corner of the nation and the globe. They bring with them different languages and cultures, different religions and backgrounds and politics and views of the world.

The personal quests that call them to this country are many and varied but they all come with expectation and excitement and with one experience in mind – to see the rock.

Ayers Rock. Uluru.

For some it's a holiday, for others a pilgrimage. For some it's a destination. For many it's a journey. They come to connect. They come to disconnect.

Some are here to scratch the itch of adventure, enticed by the slickly promoted vision of a vast and extreme frontier experience.

Some have come to pit themselves against the elements and conquer a challenge. Some will choose to climb the rock. More and more will not.

Lured by the promise of a glimpse into Australia's spiritual and physical core, they bring their families, their children, their lovers, their friends. Some are honeymooners, others are ticking their way through a bucket list of late-life must-dos.

Some come with the plaintive hope that the answers to life's great questions lie somewhere here in the ancient heart of a nation.

They come seeking salve for wounded souls. They come in search of some kind of spiritual glue with which to seal a gaping hole left by their own retreating faith.

They come yearning for connection to the oldest continuous culture on earth or they come simply to try to better understand the mysterious indigenous soul of this continent, a soul from which they have too long felt detached.

Some come to heal, others to party. For many, it's a place to learn and for others it's a place to teach. For some it's another stop on a whirlwind, follow-the-flag rattle around the world before time runs out.

Some are here to capture the rock on canvas, on film or in their mind's eye. Most will immortalise their time here through social media's filter. Others will try to write about it and wonder how they could so quickly run out of superlatives.

There are scientists answering the siren call of the geological marvel of the largest single monolith on earth, and astronomers and astrologers who come to gaze into the infinite night skies in search of celestial revelations and cosmic truth.

And many simply want to see the iconic natural wonder that's been embedded for generations in the Australian psyche.

Whatever the motivation, more than a quarter of a million will visit this year alone and most – not all, but most – will come with good intentions and an open heart.

• • • •

From a bench in the meagre shade of the tall gallery wall, two old men watch as the minga (a word they use for tourists meaning, literally, ants) come and go, scurrying to and fro with barely a glance in the men's direction.

Those who do notice the pair seem to glance only fleetingly at a couple of old, garden variety Aboriginals looking much like they've been placed there to enrich the authenticity of the tourists' visit to the central desert.

Beneath the brims of their hats – one a well-worn Akubra, the other a natty little straw trilby – the men's eyes, squinted as they have been for decades against the relentless desert sun, move languidly back and forth as the procession continues.

There is no resentment in those eyes, just a weary bemusement at the constant stream of visitors to their country. The men, two brothers, are all but invisible to the parade of visitors who have come to pay homage, for whatever reason, to Uluru.

They see the minga; the minga don't see them.

And the minga don't see the irony of an opportunity lost as they hurry past the brothers, either to get their first up-close-and-personal view of Uluru or to download their photos once they return.

It is tempting but unfair to pitch blame in any direction.

There are those among the throngs of blissfully unaware tourists who do indeed glance in the direction of the brothers, and of those there are some who break their step just long enough to signal a fleeting temptation to approach.

But the sacredness of an ancient traditional culture that has necessarily kept the curious at arm's length can give even the most inquiring and well-intentioned of casual visitors pause to fear an approach might be deemed intrusive.

Others simply don't know what they don't know. They neither know nor care to ask.

Either way, it clenches the heart to realise these men are accustomed to the periphery. Used to dwelling on the fringe. Familiar with the disconnect between those who visit, those who live here and those whose families have been here for tens of thousands of years.

Because the minga will all say they've come to see Uluru but if they were to pause a moment and ask these brothers, Reggie and Cassidy, "Who are you?", each of the men would tell them:

"I AM Uluru."

CHAPTER 1

—

Mutitjulu murder: the first shot

Atila (Mt Conner) October, 1934

Imalyangu heard the beast before he saw it.

He cocked his head towards the strange clinking sound, motioning instinctively for his three companions to be still.

Through the smoke of the campfire, a hulking horned creature moved slowly towards them, its head lowered, a talisman – the source of the unfamiliar sound – swinging from its neck.

The men leapt and yelped in fright, pedalling backwards in the red sand of the dune as the mamu (evil spirit) neared.

Clawing in the dirt for their spears, Imalyangu and his brother Yukun* slowed their breath and, steadily drawing their arms back, took aim at the beast.

As the razor-sharp spear heads lodged in its flank, the creature let out an unearthly bellow and fled into the gathering desert dusk, leaving the startled foursome in its wake.

The men had been out hunting on Atila country and had made camp for the night when the beast approached. Now, as he stared into the gloom from which the mamu had appeared, Imalyangu was uneasy – not only because of the encounter with the strange creature.

Since the arrival of piranpa (white people), so much had begun to change. Tjukurpa, which since the dawn of time had set down an ordered and unchallenged way of life for Anangu, made no accommodation for the curious and troubling ways of the pale skinned intruders.

Imalyangu's father, to whom the newcomers mistakenly referred as Lungkata**, had been among the first Anangu to encounter the peculiar visitors, telling of unfamiliar language, strange tucker and animals that were stranger still.

Piranpa seemed to need to give everyone a name instead of identifying people by their country or Tjukurpa, as did Anangu. They called Imalyangu "Paddy". It was a name that sat like an ill-fitting skin but one the whitefella history books would forever record as his. The piranpa came with guns and men they called police, and an altogether foreign and frightening way of relating to each other and to the land. And, most ominous of all, to Anangu.

Peering into the darkness in the wake of the fleeing creature, Imalyangu's unease grew and plans for the celebratory feast after a successful hunt were abandoned. The men snuffed out their fire, swept the area clear and turned back to walk through the night to the settlement where other Anangu were camped near what the piranpa called Mount Conner. The four walked in unsettled silence, peering nervously around the otherwise so familiar bush for any sign of the returning mamu.

They reached the settlement just as the sun began to float up over the horizon, listening as they approached to the tjiplis (old men) calling between camps, broadcasting the night's news and the day's plans.

Imalyangu didn't hear the blow coming. The rifle butt cracked the back of his head, bringing him to his knees as he looked up into the flaming eyes of a policeman silhouetted menacingly against the morning sky.

"You thieving black bastards!" roared the man in English, a language Imalyangu didn't understand.

Yukun and the other two had been similarly felled and were trying to shield themselves from the hail of rifle blows.

"Wiya! Wiya! (No! No!)," they shouted, struggling to find both their feet and any words of defence. It was useless. The four were dragged to a nearby tree at gunpoint, protesting desperately but futilely while bewildered Anangu watched the commotion in fearful impotence.

As the sun moved across the sky, the chains around the men's necks began to burn but it was the fire of frustration and fear that smouldered most fiercely in Imalyangu's belly. With the help of an Anangu man who spoke a little English, the four had pieced together both the charge against them and their coming fate.

The creature they had speared, thinking it was mamu, belonged to the piranpa station owner – a milking cow – and Imalyangu, his brother and their two companions stood accused of trying to kill and eat the creature, which had instead found its way back to the station with two tell-tale spears dangling from its side.

Piranpa looked unkindly, to say the least, on what they called "stealing", a term foreign to Anangu who had no concept of ownership beyond sacred traditional knowledge. For Anangu, everything – from the sky to the land and all the people and plants and animals on it – belonged to Tjukurpa, and therefore to everyone. Anangu way was to share. Not so for piranpa whose wrath knew no bounds when it came to the appropriation, intentional or otherwise, of what they considered their property.

Imalyangu knew he and Yukun and their friends would soon feel the full force of that fury and, without English words, could do little to defend themselves.

He wondered what difference a grasp of this strange language would make, anyway. The men had heard the stories that spread across country like a storm of dust – tales of Anangu bound and whipped and killed without mercy by skittish piranpa who needed but feared the ancient ways of the black skinned people with whom they shared a quest for survival in the central deserts of Australia.

With Imalyangu's ill-fitting new name, Paddy, came an equally ill-fitting sense that a swift and dangerous shift was coming to bring change to an ordered Anangu world that had remained unbroken since the creation beings formed the land and its laws. And this man, Paddy, knew that as surely as the blazing sun would soon dip below the horizon, he and his three fellow captives would not see it rise again if they could not escape the chains that held them.

As night fell, Paddy spoke to the others, not with words but through the gentle exercise of ancient, silent hand gestures.

"Be still. Hush. Wait."

When the moon was high in the sky and the sounds of the piranpa camp had settled, Paddy bent his head carefully so as not to disturb the chains that bound the men to each other. Pushing his long fingers deep into his beard, he worked free a small piece of wire he'd found and hidden there.

Instinct guided the sliver of metal into the lock next to his ear, and he listened intently for a small click of release. The lock swung open, and Paddy grabbed at his neck to still the chain as it fell. Working quickly, he freed his stunned companions, motioning them to silence.

For eternal minutes they waited for the rush of piranpa footsteps they feared, but the quiet of the camp was unbroken. The men carefully and soundlessly laid down the hated chains and with the stealth of the feather-footed kutatji, crept out into the darkness and towards the heart of their country.

Paddy knew a pursuit would be mounted once the escape was discovered, so on and on through the night the four men jogged, each footstep carefully placed atop a button of tjanpi (spinifex) so as to disguise their trail.

By the time the sun raised its head behind them, the four were exhausted but fear compelled them towards the sacred place of their ancestors, Uluru. As the great rock rose up on the horizon ahead, Paddy chanced a glance back to the east and saw a plume of red dust, rising like a devil from the plain behind them.

Piranpa. On horseback.

The four began to hum, their voices rising in a low rumbling chant as they ran, singing*** the pursuing horses to ease their pace.

Uluru rose up and up ahead but the swirl of the pursuers' dust rose higher still behind them and as the four reached the base of the great rock, Paddy could feel the terrifying thump of hooves on the earth of this most sacred of ground.

A sharp sound split the air and Yukun gasped in shock beside his brother. The shot from a policeman's rifle had found its mark in his shoulder and he stumbled, a dark stain blooming against his black skin like the sap from the bloodwood tree he grasped as he fell.

Paddy reached for his brother, dragging the injured man to his feet and urging him on towards the safety of the rocks at the base of Uluru, where they had played as children. If they could just reach the cave above Mutitjulu waterhole, the men could shelter from their pursuers and invoke the ancient spirit of Kuniya, the python woman who had waged a mighty battle there to protect her family.

Together, Paddy and the others clambered up over the red boulders they knew so well, carrying his bleeding brother into the cave as the police party halted at the base of the rock, shouting threats and demanding surrender.

To the men's dismay, they had seen a black man among the police party – a tracker engaged by the piranpa to hunt down his fellow Anangu – and Paddy's heart clenched at the power of whitefella ways to challenge ancient Tjukurpa.

From their position in the cave, the men could see the police party below and knew it would only be a matter of time before the bullets would again find them. Pushing aside their fear, the men summoned their last reserves of strength and courage to attempt a dash across the steep face of the rock to a higher cave, the depth of which would allow them shelter from the deadly rifles.

"Wiya," whispered Yukun. "I will not make it."

"Uwa (yes) you will, brother," Paddy urged him, wondering as he spoke if it were a lie.

With a rush, the men burst from the crevice and flung themselves upwards towards the safety of the higher cavern, the sudden movement catching the police party by surprise.

But the lapse was momentary and as Paddy reached down from the mouth of the deeper cave to haul his wounded brother to safety, a dreadful crack echoed through the folds of Uluru like the wail of a grieving mother.

Yukun was suddenly still. His grasp loosened and he slid heavily, his lifeblood leaving a stain both on the great red rock's flank and Paddy's heart as it followed his brother's descent to the base of the Uluru.

There was nothing the three men could do. Paddy knew that to show themselves would bring the same fate, but the torment of hearing his brother's dying voice would stay with him forever.

The police made no move to retrieve the body, instead firing intermittently at the mouth of the cave while building a fire in a futile effort to smoke the three men from their hiding. The depth and darkness of the cavern held Paddy and his friends safe for now but Paddy knew they could not stay forever in the bosom of Uluru, at least not physically.

He crept to the edge of the cave and watched as the police and their tracker made camp at the base of the rock near the waterhole, determined to await their fugitives' eventual surrender.

But the powerful presence of Uluru eventually lulled the piranpa and their Anangu tracker to sleep and when the moon was overhead, Paddy and the two other men crept from the mouth of the rock, making not a sound as they crabbed their way to the ground below.

The lifeless form of his brother was as a spear to his heart but he could do nothing now to help Yukun and Paddy's tears fell as silently as his footsteps as, like spirits, the three men slid unheeded past the snoring piranpa.

When Paddy reached the outline of the sleeping Anangu betrayer's head, he paused. As he raised the lethal weight of the large rock he had scooped up as he left the cave, one of the piranpa horses stirred, its snuffling like a siren call in the still of the Uluru darkness. Paddy lowered the rock. Tjukurpa's demand**** that his brother's death be avenged would have to wait.

With the moon now moving lower in the clear, star-studded sky, the men again sprinted soundlessly away into the darkness, only this time they were three. And this time, they would run across country and they would not stop.

As he ran, Imalyangu glanced back at the imposing outline of the great rock, silhouetted against a night sky studded with the eyes of the creation beings watching his progress out into the desert and away from this place. The place of his father. His people. His Tjukurpa. His country. This was his place. Uluru was his, and he was Uluru.

He couldn't know it then, but it would be many, many seasons, almost a lifetime, before he – now Paddy Uluru – would see it again.

● ● ● ●

* *In official reports from the time, Paddy's brother's name is recorded as Yokunnuna, however the Uluru family say it was more likely Yukun. This discrepancy may arise from the fact that Anangu culture decrees that the name of a deceased person not be mentioned for a time deemed appropriate by the family. In the case of Paddy's brother his name has rarely, if ever, been enunciated since his death. For Anangu, the relationship with another is far more important than the name.*

** *Lungkata was the name given to the Anangu man and his family (two wives and three children, but likely before Imalyangu/Paddy was born) encountered near Uluru in the late 1800s by early anthropologists W.B. Spencer and F.J. Gillen. Spencer and Gillen recorded in their 1912 diaries having met a man called Lungkatitukukana in 1894 but it is almost certain the man identified himself to the visitors not by name but by his Tjukurpa, as is the Anangu way. To this day, Anangu will more likely identify or introduce themselves (or even answer the phone) by their country or their totem or their place, rather than by their name as would piranpa. Lungkata Tjukurpa is the blue-tongue lizard dreaming, but Spencer and Gillen understandably believed this was the man's name. There is no record or recollection of Paddy's father's Anangu birth name. He is instead recorded by history as Lungkata. Family lore has it that in 1873, Paddy's father also met the early explorer William Gosse, largely credited with what we now call "first contact" and believed to be the first white man to see (or at least document seeing) Uluru, which he named in honour of then Chief Secretary of South Australia, Sir Henry Ayers.*

*** *The practice of "singing" someone is widely associated, by white interpretation at least, with the imposition of a deadly curse or with "pointing the bone". It is true that the kutatji men (traditional "executioners") would often "sing" their victim and to be sung, for Anangu who hold to traditional beliefs, can indeed be a death sentence. However, people can also be sung for more benign reasons – for a lost love, for someone who is missing or far away, to bring someone home or to make a particular event come true. The women of Kaltukatjara (Docker River) community, for instance, made a sweet offer to me during a discussion of women's business – "We will sing you up a grandchild!" In piecing together the jigsaw of the story of the shooting at Uluru, we were told of* how the four men had "sung the horses tired ones" to slow their pursuers' progress.

**** Under traditional law, Tjukurpa, any serious transgression can be punishable by either death or injury, depending on the severity of the crime. The punishment is usually dictated by the senior initiated men in what westerners might interpret as "tribal council". Often, the transgressor is speared with such precision (mostly in the leg) so as to cause injury but not death and many Anangu still bear the scars of the imposition of this traditional practice. For more serious offences, such as the revelation of sacred-secret knowledge, for desecrating sacred ground or for the unlawful killing of fellow Anangu, the punishment is death. This punishment can be meted out many seasons after the offence and can be visited on the descendants of the original transgressor.

The betrayal of Paddy and the other three by the Anangu man – whose name is reported to have been, fatefully, Carbine – was a crime of just such magnitude.

In retelling their particular version of the story, members of the Uluru family told of Paddy's intention to kill the sleeping Carbine until he was thwarted by the "snoring" of a horse. They told also of how, upon his return to Uluru from "exile" in the 1950s, Anangu living near the rock were still fearful that Paddy would search for some way to "square 'im back" – to avenge his brother's death – even more than two decades after the shooting.

An account of the incident by Joseph Donald, one of the four men, was recorded by David Batty at Kaltukatjara (Docker River) in 1986 (published on YouTube by Rebel Films in 2016), prior to the death of Donald who was the last survivor. During this account, Donald speaks of payback:

"I thought, I'm going to get that Carbine. He's a Nyangatjatjara bloke. The others said they were going to shoot him."

The practice of payback is, by its nature, secret and sacred according to Tjukurpa. Although rumours of payback abound to this day across the central and western desert regions, and there is evidence aplenty to suggest the consequences of breaking traditional law are still very much a part of Anangu society, neither the punishment nor its application is talked about outside the circle of those charged by Tjukurpa to impose it.

So, as is right under traditional law, the truth of what happened or didn't happen to Carbine, or indeed to any of his descendants or associates, will only ever be known by those who hold that sacred knowledge.

· · · ·

The story of the shooting at Uluru in 1934 has been told and retold around campfires and boiling billies across the vast reaches of the Ngaanyatjarra Pitjantjatjara Yankunytjatjara (NPY) lands for four generations. It is told still, with an intoxicating mix of reverence, regret and bewilderment.

The death of Yukun and Paddy's subsequent flight from his spiritual homeland is a seminal moment in the story of the Uluru family, for it in effect marks the point at which the fight for the handback of the land from whitefellas began its slow burn.

But in the many retellings the story has morphed, as family sagas tend to do, into a tale whose precise details are cloudy at best.

There are a number of reasons for this.

That Anangu history and lore are oral, rather than written, renders a whitefella-style search for the "official" account from the family's perspective utterly futile. Such a search instead yields mostly those accounts documented by observers and the authorities of the time, and these accounts diverge markedly from both each other and from the story told by the Uluru family itself.

Some records have it that the four men had been charged under Tjukurpa with the task of meting out traditional punishment on a fellow tribesman for the deeply offensive crime of revealing sacred knowledge to his woman. The four came to the attention of the piranpa authorities because they carried out this punishment using a rifle rather than traditional Anangu methods, not for the killing itself which was an imperative demanded by Tjukurpa, and to fail in this task would be to themselves break sacred law and suffer the same fate.

And herein lies perhaps the most compelling reason for what the distant observer might see as a refinement of the truth. The truth is that the story has shifted shape not so as to re-write history, but to protect it.

Even the most peripheral discussion of sacred business and secret law is fraught, particularly in a changing world where judgement is made through the prism of western culture. For initiated Anangu to discuss or refer to traditional business, even in the most superficial terms, is to risk the revelation of knowledge that must be protected under Tjukurpa, and this is a shameful crime according to Anangu law.

Through discussions with members of the Uluru family and the wider Anangu community, it became clear on a number of occasions that many an ancient creation story has been sanitised for consumption by a wider public than the ancestral figures or even early 20th century elders could ever have foreseen.

Even some of the most widely known of the Anangu dreaming or creation stories have been given a little whitewash to ensure their smooth passage across a cultural divide. Some of the real creation stories are the stuff of nightmares, filled with brutal and violent warnings and examples to those who ignore Tjukurpa or do not heed the lessons set down therein.

If indeed the "official" accounts of the circumstances surrounding the shooting of Paddy Uluru's brother in the shadow of that great and sacred rock have any truth, in the whitefella sense, is it any wonder these truths have been passed over in favour of a gentler and safer retelling?

Even though the murder of Paddy's brother is a key event in the Uluru history, and even though the story is still very much a part of Anangu consciousness, the tale has never been included in the patter for tourists who visit Mutitjulu Waterhole. Of the hundreds of visitors who take the guided Kuniya walk tour every day, none has ever heard this story from the lips of an Anangu guide.

It is often said that history is written by the victor, and if that holds true the Uluru family is wise to keep its own truths close and sacred.

Readers are welcome to elsewhere explore the documented historical landscape in order to satisfy their curiosity, but the above is the story as told by the Uluru family itself and pieced together with the help of some necessary but gentle creative license.

• • • •

Reggie Uluru sits cross legged under the low, scrubby branches of a mulga tree in the fine red dust of his father Paddy's old camp near Mutitjulu, at the eastern flank of the rock. In concert with Alan Wilson, another member of the extended family*, he speaks of the shooting of his uncle, whose name has not been uttered for the best part of a century:

> The story was that they saw this thing they thought was some kind of scary monster – a devil, for all they knew. This thing with horns on its head. It was a milking cow, but they didn't know that. They speared it, and because they'd speared it, it limped back to the station shed (Mt Conner) to the water.
>
> There were a number of them involved, four of them. My father and his brother and two others. They were chained up together. The whitefella, when he saw the milking cow with the spear in it, he got really wild and got his gun. He said, "I'm going to kill you all!"
>
> The four men escaped. The men had broken off some of the chains. They had cut themselves separately so they could run. They were chased by the whitefellas, and the police also used a black-tracker.
>
> They came back to Uluru. They ran and ran and ran. They were racing all the way, over sand dunes and all this country, and following them were all the horses. But the horses got worn out because the men had sung the horses. They had sung those horses tired ones.
>
> When they got to Uluru, they hid in a cave. One of them – Paddy's brother – was shot in the shoulder as they were climbing up to hide in the cave.
>
> They didn't have a spear or spears, otherwise they would have been able to spear the pursuers but he (Paddy's brother) got a club and hurled it at one of the policemen and the black tracker (the police aide who was with them) shot Paddy's

brother in the shoulder.

They didn't stop – they just kept running.

They ran into that first cave but it was too shallow and the men realised the police could still shoot them so they decided to move further up the rock to another cave that was deeper.

The wounded man was weak. They all went into the cave but they had to leave him because he was so weak from the wound. He couldn't climb up into the cave – he was too weak. They knew they would be okay in the back of the cave but the wounded man couldn't make it – he was slower – and the policemen shot him again.

The other men should have been able to get him into the cave, to help him but they were too scared to go out and get him to bring him into the safety of the cave. They were all single men. They were wati (young fella) with no children.

The dying man was yelling out "Help me!" "Come and get me!" but they were too scared. That made them feel bad. They were crying inside the cave because they were too frightened to go out and help their friend (Paddy's brother) because they knew if they did they too would be shot.

Then the police tried to smoke them out of the cave by setting fire to the bush, but they were really far inside that deeper cave.

This was at the Rainbow Serpent's place and there was water inside the cave. They were waiting for the Rainbow Serpent to attack.

The policemen got tired while they were waiting for the men to come out of the cave and they went to sleep. They gave up waiting.

Then the men crept out in the middle of the night – perhaps it was midnight – and they were very quiet. They didn't have spears, otherwise they would have speared the sleeping policemen but instead they got a big rock. They were about to use the rock to kill the sleeping men to pay them back, when one of the horses snored and they were worried the horses stirring might wake the policemen.

So they ran. They were so frightened for their lives. And they ran and ran and ran. They left Uluru and the Mutitjulu waterhole and they ran away. They went out west and then left one of the men who kept going west, and the other two men (including Paddy) went south into South Australia, around Ernabella.

We often wonder if anyone ever went back to get Paddy's brother. Did someone go back to get the bones and bury him? We don't know. No-one ever talks about this.

There was no-one, no Anangu at Uluru at the time. The men just fled in fear. But this was Paddy's homeland and it would have been very hard for him to leave.

Along the way, they killed a perentie but nearly choked on the lizard because they were so dry (in the mouth) because they had not had any water. They were so hungry they had to eat but I remember my father telling me about nearly choking on the meat because their mouths were so dry from dehydration.

(Paddy) went right away to the east eventually and got married. When he came back to Uluru, there were not many people here. They had all gone out to Kaltukatjara (Docker River). I think maybe they were frightened because of what happened to my father when his brother was shot.

People would say, "Come back to your home country (Uluru) but they would say, "No, I'm still frightened." That's because of what happened.

Some were frightened of my father and ran away. They wouldn't sit down in their family groups. They were frightened because they thought my father might spear them because everyone knew he'd lost his brother here and he might be looking to square'em back with someone for that death.

Maybe people were thinking my father might be looking to get payback for his brother's death – scared that someone might have to take the blame for that death. But that wasn't right.

· · · ·

In the lead-up to the handback of Uluru-Kata Tjuta in 1985, a number of submissions that were made to the inquiry in support of the land claim made mention of the shooting at the rock, including this excerpt from a submission written by Reverend Jim Downing for the Uniting Church in refuting the then Northern Territory government's assertion that the area had historically been uninhabited by Anangu:

> *In 1934 Paddy Uluru, recognised by Pitjantjatjara and Yankunytjatjara people as the number one custodian of Uluru, was deputised with his brother and others to execute a young man who had betrayed deep ceremonial secrets and an important sacred site to his girlfriend. Strehlow[1] recorded the story and said that if the men had killed the offender in the traditional manner, white people in the area would have taken no notice at all, but they borrowed a rifle from a white station owner who lived with an Aboriginal woman near Mt Conner. That frightened white people in the district and the police were called in. They chained Paddy and his fellows together. During the night, Paddy picked the locks with a piece of wire he had found and hidden in his beard. They escaped and made a forced march toward Uluru. On the way the police party caught up and Paddy's brother was shot but managed to escape.*
>
> *The men reached Uluru and were resting at the cave at Maggie Springs (Mutitjulu Waterhole) when the police came upon them. Uluru's brother was shot again, this time fatally. He called to Uluru, who had hidden in the recesses of the cave, "I'm finished. They'll get you too. Take the sacred things and leave this place and go to a far country."*
>
> *After the police had gone, the men buried Uluru's brother. Uluru then hid the sacred objects at the rock and they left the area.*
>
> - Excerpt from Uluru: A National Park for All Australians or a National Tragedy – Jim Downing, 1984-1985, a manuscript from the Bill Edwards collection held by Ara Irititja.

In the retelling, the Uluru family makes no mention of sacred objects or of burying Yukun, saying instead that the mystery of what happened to the slain man's body remained a painful thorn in Paddy's side until his own death in 1979.

This is not unusual, given that if there were indeed sacred objects – perhaps reclaimed from the man the four had been sent to punish – they were and are just that, sacred, and the knowledge of them and what happened to them should not, and need not, be discussed. The same could be said of discussion of Yukun's body, given the depth of spirituality that goes with death for Anangu.

Neither is any mention made, even in the recorded account by Joseph Donald, who was the last surviving member of the party of four fugitives, of any trial or of being brought before whitefella court.

A newspaper report[2] of the trial of the police officer charged with the shooting further clouds the story, but leaves a trail for the interested reader to follow and offers some insight into the attitude of some authorities of the day:

> In a case of the murder of a native which came before Judge Wells in the Supreme Court of the Northern Territory sitting in Alice Springs today, Mounted Constable McKinnon, of the Northern Territory south west patrol, admitted that in self-defence he had shot a native prisoner who had escaped custody and was resisting arrest. He denied further allegations that natives were flogged to obtain admissions of guilt.

The article quotes the crown as describing the accused as "semi-civilised natives" who had been given a gun, by a white man named Hughes, with which to hunt euro (small kangaroo) around Mt Conner and had instead shot another native whose "lubra"** had found his body some time later. The killing was reported to police during their next patrol.

In the report, a number of Anangu names are mentioned in reference to the accused but in another illustration of the difficulty in ascertaining precise details of this or any other events in turn-of-the-century and early 1900s central Australia, none of these names is Imalyangu, or Paddy's.

Mr B.N. Webb, counsel for the accused put to Constable McKinnon a number of accusations including that these "semi-civilised natives" had been beaten, dragged by their hair and had dogs sooled on them while they lay unconscious. McKinnon denied all allegations of violence or mistreatment.

> *Webb: Why did you shoot Yokununna (Yukun)?*
> *McKinnon: He was in a cave with a low, narrow entrance. I called to him several times. A stone flew past my head and another hit my hand.*
> *Webb: As a result of that awful assault, you had to fire to save your life?*
> *McKinnon: I did not know how he was armed. I never saw him in the open.*
> *Webb: How did you know he was there?*
> *McKinnon: I smelt him and a tracker tracked him.*

With the help of an interpreter, the wife of the man who was allegedly shot with the white man's gun gave evidence and was described somewhat patronisingly to the court as "an intelligent lubra". By contrast, a medical practitioner who was also Deputy Chief Protector of Aborigines, told the court "he would estimate that the intellect of the average adult Aborigine to be on the level with that of a boy of fourteen years".

When the authorities' enquiry into the shooting wound to a close in September 1935, the finding was that while the shooting was not warranted, it was justifiable under the law. The piranpa law.

What IS clear is that the death of his brother at the hands of the authorities drove the man who would become widely acknowledged as the patriarch of the modern Uluru family into fearful exile for more than twenty years.

When his yearning for Uluru finally brought Paddy back to his spiritual home, he brought with him the sons and the genesis of a family that would eventually see it returned, in the way of the whitefella, to the people it had belonged to, and them to it, since the dawn of time.

· · · ·

Alan Wilson is "uncle" to Sammy Wilson (whitefella way) but is father for Sammy because Alan is the brother of Sammy's father. The term for a man who "grew you up" is mama-nyuyurpa.

**Lubra is a word meaning "woman" that comes from elsewhere in Australia — not the Central Desert regions — and was used almost exclusively by white people. The term is not often used now because of its paternalistic overtones.*

1. Professor TGH Strehlow, an anthropologist and linguist who lived and worked in Central Australia and who, through his connection with Anangu, took part in the 1935 Committee of Inquiry that visited Uluru to investigate Yokununna's death.
2. The Adelaide Advertiser, February 11, 1935 – State Library of South Australia

CHAPTER 2

—

"A big story, that one"

In the soft red earth of the birthing place, the minyma (women) gathered around the exhausted young mother. The tjitji (child) was still; thin and unmoving as they gently turned the tiny form over and over. Finally, softly, its chest rose with the first breath of desert air.[*]

They could hear the sounds of the men's camp floating distantly across the dunes on the searing afternoon air, and the women exchanged glances.

It had been many suns since rain had fallen and the landscape, and life on it, was as unforgiving as the spirits themselves. A child needed to be strong from its first gasp. The ancestral beings had weakened this woman and her baby with such a hard season. Perhaps they intended for this child to return to them to await rebirth in more favourable times.

Among the minyma huddled around the mother's heaving body, one set of eyes watched intently as the others parted the child's legs. A boy.

She looked down at the baby, still glistening wet from his journey into the world.

No, this tjitji would not live. She would see to it.

Darkness had long since settled over the camp and the slice of moon was high overhead when the woman – a wife to the father of the scrawny new-born – crept to where the child lay cradled in the warmth of his piti[**]. His mother slept, wearied from the birth and the long months of carrying new life inside her.

The infant stirred but made no sound as the woman gently slid her fingers into his mouth, leaving there a pinch of mingkulpa.[***] His dark eyes stared up into hers but the woman felt no remorse. This was how it must be. The sedative effect of the bush tobacco would ease his journey back to the spirits.

She retreated to her earthen bed beyond the dying coals of the fire, watching for a long time before sleep overcame her. In the morning, she hoped, the mingkulpa would add weight to the proclamation that the family could not withstand the burden of a sickly child.

From across the camp, another set of eyes also watched.

As the sun cracked across the horizon, slowly warming the desert night's chill, the mother looked down into the face of her son and knew what the day would hold for them both. It was as it needed to be. She would not grieve her child. She would do as Tjukurpa bid and surrender her son to the spirits.

Her husband's other wife, confident her nocturnal ministrations had gone unseen, plucked the baby from its coolamon. His little body was pale and limp, his black eyes blank with drowsiness.

"I will do what needs to be done."

Without hesitation, she carried the baby away into the bush, the eyes of the minyama following her without emotion. Once she could no longer see the camp behind her the woman knelt, resting the child on the ground. Her hands worked quickly, digging into the earth until the hole was big enough to swallow the tiny life lying listlessly beside her.

Placing him into the meagre grave, she buried the softly breathing little brown form, handful by handful, under the fine red soil of his ancestors and walked back to camp without looking back.

But the one whose eyes had seen all had followed the older woman's footsteps and, as those footsteps now retreated, rushed from her hiding place behind the thatch of mulga trees and dropped to her knees beside the forlorn little mound.

Clawing frantically, she cleared the shroud of dirt from the baby's face, scraping the lethal pall from his nostrils and mouth. He was breathing. Pukulpa. He would live.

The woman whose jealousy had nearly sent the tiny boy to his death shot to her feet as the kungka (young woman) strode back into the camp with the child nestled against her chest.

Shock gave way to rage.

"Do you know what you have done, kungka?" she growled, her

eyes blazing like the coals of a campfire. "That child is sick. You are rama-rama (mad)!"

The girl knew exactly what she had done and met the older woman's gaze with an accusing stare of her own. The woman looked away, searching in vain for support in the faces of the minyma and the woman who had borne the child. None came.

The voice of a grandmother stilled the air between the two women.

"The choice has been made," said the minyma-pampa (elderly woman), raising her hand to hush any further recriminations. "You take this burden because you are now this child's mother."

It was as it was. The kungka would now be the tjitji's mother. It was done.

The kungka looked down into the eyes of the child. Her brother. Son of her mother. Now her son. She would care for him. She would keep him safe. She would grow him up. She and the child would take each sunrise as it came. Tjukurpa would guide them both.

"Uwa," she cooed. "My tjitji."

She placed the tip of her little finger into her new son's mouth and smiled at his strong sucking reflex.

The child looked up into the eyes of the woman he would come to know as mother and clenched his tiny fists, ready even then to do battle for his place in the world.

• • • •

Reggie Uluru doesn't know how old he is. He just knows he's been around "long time – long, long time".

Age is a whitefella concern. Numbers don't matter. He is tjilpi (wise old man). He is tjamu (grandfather). He is Uluru. That's what matters.

Without specific records, his family's best reckoning is that Tjamu Reggie has been around for more than eighty summers, give or take.

His recollections come, not chronologically for that is the way of the whitefella, but in the order in which he senses the listener needs and is ready to hear them. True to Tjukurpa, and to the broader Anangu way, information is dispensed on what westerners might call a "need to know" basis. This is neither conceit nor churlish superiority, it is simply that for thousands of years the dissemination of knowledge was, by necessity, precisely timed to maximise its value.

To give knowledge and information to those for whom it has no practical application is to potentially dilute the knowledge and information that IS needed for survival.

And so it was with Tjamu Reggie's contemporary telling of his own story. He was able to intuit my readiness to receive information, regardless of my barely contained but premature curiosity.

Over many visits and many conversations Reggie offered snippets and glimpses into his eighty-something year journey so far. He spoke in general terms of his childhood, of his working life, of his family, of hunting and walking country, of incidents and experiences and recollections.

However, it was only with the passage of nearly three years of "interviews" (in whitefella parlance) and with my herculean efforts at patience, that he sensed my readiness to hear some of the more intimate details of his life. Only once he was confident I would hear and process these stories and information without judgement and in the context of all the cumulative knowledge he had already passed on – the laying of the cross-cultural foundations, as it were – did he tell of the circumstances surrounding his birth.

Even with those foundations laid, his words were stunning in the deepest sense of the term:

> My mother didn't grow me up. She ran off with another man a long time ago from my birthplace at Paramita. A sister for me, she was the one who grew me up.
>
> When I was born it was drought time, a hard time. Maybe that is why I was a really skinny new-born. Maybe I was not expected to survive.
>
> They buried me because they didn't think I was going to live anyway.

This is something that people would do (in the old days). If there were two wives, or one husband or a promised one, and a man was married to his woman and she had a baby – this other one, through the jealousy, would maybe give the new-born baby some bush tobacco (mingkulpa) to poison the child and then say, "Oh your child is really skinny, really sickly" and actually, through that jealousy, kill that child.

I think that's what happened to me, but I was alright. My sister dug me up. She was an older sister for me, from the same country. And so she grew me up. She became my mother.

I was not fed by the breast, there was no wet nurse. They fed me with nanny-goat milk. This was at Amuroona (near where I was born) and there was already a station there and they had goats, so they used that nanny goat milk to feed me.

I remember that place; that place where I was buried. I can show you. I will show you one day.

My mum – the one who born me – she ran away with another man. Long time ago.

She ran away with this other man and I ended up with her other daughter who dug me up – my sister who was working on the station. She must have had some English (language).

Nothing was ever said (to the authorities about me being buried as a baby). My mother (sister in whitefella way) said not to tell what really happened to me. She said maybe it wouldn't be too good to let people know that story. She thought that maybe people knowing that story might give them ideas and some people might do the same thing. Maybe if someone is not giving them money or something like that, they might decide to poison that person.

I don't often tell that story.

That's a big story, that one.

• • • •

That infanticide was until relatively recently practiced by traditional Anangu and other indigenous Australian communities, in fact almost universally in early societies around the globe, is anathema to the modern observer regardless of ethnicity. There is arguably no ancient society on earth that did not exercise infanticide to some extent or in some form, but as with so much of Anangu cultural history, the practice needs to be viewed in context of the environmental and social construct of the times.

While the story of Reggie Uluru's burial at birth introduces elements of arguably the worst of human traits, as a generalisation the practice of infanticide was not motivated by a disregard for human life but, perverse as it sounds, more often with a regard to preserving it.

This is hard for the contemporary onlooker to fathom. That Reggie rarely recounts the circumstances surrounding his birth serves as another example of the way in which Anangu history may be gently sanitised so as to guard against uninformed judgement.

The reasons for the killing, directly or indirectly, of a new-born were diverse and the methods used to dispatch the ill-fated infants equally varied and never pleasant. What becomes clear though, is that in most cases the decision to kill or abandon a new-born was driven chiefly by a desire – rightly or wrongly – to either adhere to traditional law or to protect the sustainability of the larger family group. Or both.

There are accounts of babies simply being left out in the sun[1] or abandoned when the family inevitably moved camp. Some were strangled, some smothered, others buried as was the case with Reggie's nearly fatal introduction to the ruthless reality of desert life.

Further first-hand anecdotal accounts are even more distressing but a warts-and-all, in-depth description of the various methods employed to kill a baby is neither necessary nor appropriate in this forum. Suffice to say the techniques were often brutal and what we would now interpret as cruel, but almost always effective.

In particularly harsh seasons, remembering that even the mildest drought in an already unforgiving climate can be devastating, a baby who is anything but the most robust will expend precious resources, including those needed to sustain a lactating mother. Infanticide increased soon after first contact with white people, when the first mixed-race births began[2]. There are various accounts of the missionaries of the day rescuing these infants[3], while others, like Reggie, were saved from their fate by family members although this was rare and took a great deal of courage on the part of Reggie's sister.

When twins were born, one would almost always be dispatched as a matter of course as was any child born with a deformity which, to early and traditional Anangu, would likely be associated with marriage or relationships that were "wrong way", that is tribally (therefore genetically) inappropriate.

Should a woman give birth while still breast-feeding an older child, the baby – if not aborted during pregnancy – would often be sacrificed, to ensure the nourishment of the toddler through a replenished supply of breast milk.

It is hard, if not impossible, to take the emotion out of any discussion of infanticide but if one can achieve that feat, the practice of surrendering the life of a new-born to ensure the survival and endurance of the wider social group makes sense.

Humanity being the mercurial beast it is, of course there are aberrations. Reggie's story is one such example in which the motivation for infanticide may have been more sinister in nature but even jealousy is not a new concept in Anangu society.

There is a creation story, told publicly and sounding remarkably familiar, that tells of the crow and the cockatoo. It's a story of love and loss and lethal envy and a man who has two wives. One is a crow-woman, the other a cockatoo-woman. The crow woman, driven to insane jealousy by the man's attention to the cockatoo-woman, tricks her rival and eats her babies. The man discovers the tragedy and sends the crow woman to her own death.

As with all creation stories, this tale is told to underscore Tjukurpa's guidance in maintaining proper relationships within the kinship structure and in relation to the land and other Anangu. It

I AM ULURU

serves as a dire warning against the ravages of envy and jealousy.

The "crow woman" of Reggie's own story may or may not have suffered the consequences of her jealousy – we'll never know. What we do know is that his sister's remarkable courage in rescuing the scrawny tjitji has given to the world the gift of an equally remarkable and courageous soul.

• • • •

* *The first draft of this creative retelling of Reggie's birth was far more detailed in nature, the intent being to set the scene of a difficult birth. However, during the process of reading the draft for approval, the family deemed the opening paragraphs too graphic and asked that they be re-written to satisfy cultural protocol. For Anangu, the birthing process is women's business and should not be discussed, viewed or considered by men.*

** *Piti – a wooden bowl, sometimes called a "coolamon" that is traditionally used by women to carry everything from water to food to babies. These days the punu (wood) coolamons, often decorated with traditional designs and depictions through the use of a burning technique, are highly sought by tourists.*

*** *Mingkulpa – a type of bush tobacco, the effects of which are mildly narcotic. Mostly now used by older women and still much sought after today, the leaves of the mingkulpa plant are ground and mixed with the ash of certain types of native trees. Making an effective mixture is something of an art form.*

The powder is chewed to a paste just inside the lip, and the wad it yields often remains lodged, or "stored", for many hours at the side of the user's mouth. Anangu have availed themselves of this gently sedative bush tobacco for as long as anyone can remember not just for its sedative effect. It was also an effective survival tool employed during long travelling events or journeys between waterholes, thanks to its ability to suppress appetite, enhance stamina and assist with keeping the mouth hydrated.

Modern generations have tended to embrace the use of commercial tobacco products and other narcotic substances, but older Anangu, particularly the women, still favour this naturally organic product.

1. The Songkeepers – a documentary directed by Naina Sen, Brindle films 2017
2. The Original Australians: Story of the Aboriginal People – Josephine Flood, 2006 (p.120)
3. The Songkeepers – Brindle Films 2017

CHAPTER 3

–

"You take that name: Reggie"

R eggie Uluru was born in the bush near Paramita and Indulkana, sometime in the early 1930s. Despite his perilous journey into life, he grew into a robust youngster who was given the Anangu name Tjupi Tjupi.

Children are seldom given their names at birth. It is usually not until the child is around two or three years old that their Anangu name is bestowed. Most often, it is given by the child's tjamu (grandfather) and is drawn from Tjukurpa and family story line.[*]

However, little Tjupi Tjupi's whitefella name came courtesy of Molly Braeden, who was the wife of Reggie Braeden, the manager at Todd Morden Station. Reggie Uluru remembers both this lady and this time fondly as he recounts his memories.

> My Tjukurpa is emu dreaming. My dad, Paddy, was a shepherd – there was a sheep station at Granite Downs. I spent a lot of time at Todd Morden Station and I started working there as a child before I became a stockman.
>
> Molly Braeden gave me her husband's name. She said, "You take that name: Reggie." My dad (Paddy) wasn't there – I'm not sure what he was doing.
>
> I have three mothers, but Nyunmiti is my (biological) mother – her English name was Nancy. There was also Munyi, that's Cassidy's mother. We called her Munji. I can't remember Cassidy's Anangu name, I just remember him being called Cassidy. Usually a Tjamu (grandfather) gives you your name but it was his mother that gave Cassidy his name.
>
> I remember being around Wallatinna – the station – with my brothers, Andrew and Yami[**]. I think Yami and I are around the same age. We were walking, walking, hunting malu (kangaroo). In the bush as a tjitji and a young fella. I remember my grandmother used to take us out bush digging

for maku (witchetty grubs).

We were always wary of the police because my dad, Paddy, was a fugitive (since fleeing Uluru after the shooting of his brother in 1934). We spent a lot of time travelling and following old ways around the bush.

We were frightened of the police and we used to run away. We used to run away from school. That's how we ended up in Mimili – because we were running away.

When we were at Todmorden Station, my sister used to say be careful if the policemen wanted to give you something because it might be a trick, so I used to always run away. I was thinking they might put some poison in the fruit or the sweets or even in a drink they would offer you.[***]

They used to give us lollies in return for work when we were children. They would give us clothes as well. That lady, Molly Braedon, she liked the kids and she gave us work. We chopped firewood and made cement. I remember we made a base for a tank.

Molly looked after the Anangu kids. She was a good woman. She was friendly to the kids but she put us to work. Kids worked collecting fire wood and she would give us food.

Right through to teenage years I remember being on that station and doing odd jobs there. We were there, and because they liked us working around the station, they didn't like us to go off travelling to other places with other families that came through. Only when it was holiday time, only then would we go and visit other places with other families. Everyone was good to us, though. Nice and friendly.

Then we went to Mimili. I remember all the old people who were around Mimili when I was young and they were all very good people. I remember the station people being good people too. They'd ask us, "Do you want to work?" and we'd say, "Yes!" and we'd jump in the car and they'd take us off to

Despite the wealth of knowledge young Anangu learned by being out on country and walking their homelands with family, the piranpa authorities – often in the shape of missionaries – believed a whitefella education and classroom learning was more valuable.

While fluency in the English language has been of benefit in many ways, the loss of language has also been a curse for Anangu because in many cases it signals a corresponding loss of culture:

> I didn't go to school very much. I didn't like it. I ran away. White people were cranky at school. The school was at Oodnadatta – long way away from Mimili. We used to stay in the creek near Oodnadatta. I used to get on the mail truck and go back to Mimili. I didn't like school at Oodnadatta. We stayed at Mimili as a family for many years. Yami was taken away to go to school in Adelaide. But he came back eventually.
>
> Because I didn't go to school, I didn't learn too much English. But some people who learned that bible, I've already heard some of them denounce Tjukurpa.****
>
> Once I had finished my growing up – becoming a man – that's when my father brought me and my brother here to Uluru. He said, "I'm going to take you to see the range." The Anangu word is arpata, but he meant that he was bringing us to see Uluru.

The family's return to Uluru from Mimili in the late 1950s (see map on Page 122) was marked by Paddy's distress at seeing tourists desecrating sacred sites, but it would be some time before the enormity of that homecoming was recognised by Reggie and his brothers as the start of a fight for acknowledgement as traditional owners.

Reggie spent much of his youth traversing the country of his father and his ancestors, variously working for whitefellas and walking country in the traditional way. To pin-point exact timelines and events, as one would for a garden-variety biography or family story, is almost impossible given the whitefella way of chronologically gathering and recollecting information bears little relevance for Anangu.

As with much of the family's tale, the stories come in oddments that, to piranpa, seem to make little sequential sense until each of the parts are viewed as a whole. Then it becomes a multi-faceted and deeply moving picture of survival, resilience and adaptation.

Reggie worked as a cleaner, a labourer and in other roles but it was his time as a stockman that he recalls most fondly and these memories are offered in a later chapter.

Reggie also speaks with great warmth of his time as a ranger and a guide with Anangu Tours, an organisation set up and run by a largely Anangu staff to try to better inform tourists of traditional life and culture (and again, these recollections are expanded in a later chapter).

However, to give an insight into the man that is Reggie Uluru, those who knew and worked with the Uluru family during these times all speak with a deep reverence and genuine respect for not only the senior family members' knowledge and integrity, but their wisdom in understanding the value of sharing that knowledge as far as Tjukurpa will allow.

One who worked closely with Reggie is a young indigenous woman who came to the red centre from another part of Australia and gave a rare insight into the essence of Tjamu Reggie:

> "When you're around Reggie, he'll make you feel like everything you are talking about right here right now is the most important thing in the world and that what you're saying is so important – he will give you that much respect, even to a young woman. He didn't have to interact with a young woman like me, but I think it's in Reggie's character. He's very loving and giving. It's just his nature. Reggie has a very charismatic side. Women respond very well to both he and Cassidy, but particularly to Reggie. Reggie has much to teach about being a loving and giving person – he has that ability to make you forget your differences. That's not easy when you land in a place that's so different from where you came from. You can feel very much on the outside but Reggie makes you feel like you are home." [1]

To understand the importance of family to Reggie, one must remember that to Anangu, as with many other traditionally-based indigenous societies in Australia, those bonds are measured not so much by blood ties but through a complex but fundamental sense of kinship based along Tjukurpa, story and song lines.

Despite this knowledge, the temptation to default to questions based on a whitefella interpretation of family is almost impossible to overcome and Reggie is highly but gently amused by my persistent, if subconscious, focus on the who, where, when and why of various relationships. It seems he is the more accomplished of us at this compromise and does his best to put all the family players in chronological and geographical context, but says with a twinkle in his eye, "I'm just here. I'm living here."

I met my wife, Sarah (Goodwin), at Ernabella. Sarah was born somewhere around Tjayawarra (Tieyon Station) near Kulgera. We met when I was a young fella and we went travelling around. I was her second husband. She had three children before she married me.

I had two daughters and one son. They live at Indulkana now. And too many grandchildren – maybe eleven? More grandchildren than fingers!

I have lots of little uncles (great grandchildren). I'd like to go down there and spend time with them all. Or maybe they could come and visit me?

My daughter Jeannie was born on the other side of the rock (Uluru) where there's that outcrop of rock called Taputji near the airstrip. That's her birthplace. She's my first daughter. My other children Stephen and Sandra were born at Mimili.

These days, Reggie is a regular fixture in his motorised scooter around the community of Mutitjulu where he lives at the respite centre. With his signature Akubra and impressive beard, he commands a great deal of love and respect – as much, if not more, than ever. He has lost none of his gift as a raconteur and his words and stories carry enormous weight, even if his oft-injured legs no longer can.

The strings (tendons/muscles) in my right leg play up on me these days because I'm old and because of an old spear injury.

When I was at Indulkana as a wati (young man), working as a cleaner, a group of fellas had been up at Marla Bore on the drink and when they came back to Indulkana, they started a fight. I was speared during that fight. This fella was all fired up and he said, "I'm going to spear you" and I kept saying "Wiya, wiya! Don't spear me." But he threw a spear at me and it went into my thigh here. He just threw it with his hands — no throwing stick. It was quite a long spear and it had three or four barbs on each side of the tip, so it was quite a bad wound. I remember it took my breath away from me — it was like I was having a heart attack.

The Royal Flying Doctor Service flew down in the night and picked me up and took me to Alice Springs. The spear was still in my leg. They didn't want to pull it out because of the damage the barbs would do. I was in hospital for a while. I don't really know why he speared me — it was just a big fight. That's why my leg gets sore now that I am a tjilpi.

I didn't limp too badly after that, but then I had a car accident and that injured my hip. I walked with a limp after that car accident. I was driving from Coober Pedy to Mimili on the bitumen road and I thought I saw something on the road so I went like this (makes a motion of jerking the steering wheel) and the car rolled over and over. It hit a tree and I was hung up in that tree for a while. That's when my left leg was hurt, and my hip.

That's why I can't walk too well now.

I remember another time when we were driving on the road out near Curtin Springs. We were in a tray back ute. My brother was in the back of the ute and we hit a bullock. When we hit that bullock, his bowels let go and it let fly all over the tray back and shit all over my brother. Kuna (excrement/ shit) all over him! We still laugh about that one.

As the son of Paddy Uluru and the oldest member of the Uluru family, Reggie is often invited to meet with visiting dignitaries or, more precisely, those luminaries are extended the privilege of making his acquaintance.

Often there's the situation where we do inma (traditional dance) for visitors – I've danced many times over the years, not just for tourists. We've often danced for different occasions, me and my brother Cassidy.

Although some of the younger members of the family have had the opportunity to explore the world beyond their own home country and Australia's shores, Reggie has not ventured far from his vast homelands during his life. However, he has enjoyed the brief glimpses he has been able to take into the lives of other indigenous communities beyond the APY/NPY lands.

I once did a trip to the Kimberley in Western Australia. When we got there, there was a big mob to meet us. I have a photo of me with one of the traditional owners from that country who came to meet us and show us around her homeland.

Some people asked if I got homesick for my own country (while away visiting) but wiya, it's good to see other people's homelands. To see their different bush tucker and that sort of thing and to see their country.

Reggie recalls Queen Elizabeth coming to visit Uluru although, as we've come to understand is usual, he's not sure exactly which particular visit from the reigning monarch he recalls. He also met Prince Charles and his then wife Diana on their visit to the rock in 1983 and their son Prince William and his new bride Kate during their turn thirty-one years later.

As a respected elder and traditional owner, Reggie is feted by visitors but the brushes with British royalty present perhaps the most fascinating juxtaposition, given the fraught history of Anangu under colonial influence. It would be easy to imagine a resentment on the part of this wise old man who has seen so much change in his lifetime, but there is none. Not a shred of animosity. No sense of oppressed and oppressor.

The royal folk come to see Uluru and Reggie is Uluru. That's what matters.

He extends to them the same respect and care with which he welcomes all visitors to his country. They are people. People from a different homeland, with a different Tjukurpa. But they are here in this place at this time.

Long time ago, when the Queen came. When she was a kungka. I shook her hand. She's probably still alive now, eh? Thinking she might remember me, or maybe she forgot me?

He is surprised to learn that the kungka he met all those years ago has recently celebrated her ninety second birthday, that she is quite likely quite a few seasons his senior and that she is still the Queen.

We joke that if he turns 100 years old, he will get a telegram from Her Majesty. His response is pure gold:

Maybe if she is 100, I can send her a telegram, eh?

Now, wouldn't that be something?

• • • •

In placing the name with the child — placing, rather than giving, being the most accurate interpretation of the process in Anangu vernacular — the tjamu will hold the (male) child sideways across his own torso and move him back and forth, skin to skin. In this way, the tjamu is physically putting his name into his grandson. This practice is called Ngampaltjunanyi – the act of a grandfather holding his grandson. As well as placing the name, it also imparts all the grandfather's good qualities into his grandson – strength, a good eye, good judgement, kindness, generosity and so on. A child may have multiple grandfathers so he who places the name will determine the child's connection to country and Tjukurpa. That piranpa way is to bestow a name almost immediately at birth has largely interrupted this Anangu tradition, and has consequently served to change the culture and affiliation of many an Anangu child.

** Yami Lester is Reggie Uluru's cousin in the whitefella way but is called brother.

*** Three of Reggie's sisters were snatched from Mimili in 1936 when patrol officers offered the children apples and oranges as inducement. See Chapter 4: Apples and Oranges.

**** In the light of Reggie's fears for the loss of Tjukurpa to Christianity, the words of a fellow Anangu, quoted in an anthology of recollections from Aboriginal people from central Australia, are startling: "It's good to have the Christian life and to know all about Christian ways… because you know how God created the world, and it's good to learn about the world and God and Jesus and who they are and to keep teaching the young ones. God has got the most Tjukurpa." (Every Hill Got a Story; Central Land Council 2015 – p.58)

1. Interview at Mutitjulu (October 2017) with Kate Vickers, a ranger with Uluru-Kata Tjuta National Parks who worked with the Uluru family and Anangu Tours. Her insights are reproduced with permission.

CHAPTER 4

—

Apples and oranges

Mimili, 1936

By the time it rolled to a stop at the edge of the aborigines' camp, the car looked more like a moving sand-dune than a 1930s Chevrolet, its hulking, rounded bonnet and panels blanketed in the powdery red dust of the vast desert it stalked.

The driver pulled his hat onto his head, closed his eyes and steeled himself with a deep sigh. He had only been an officer with the Aborigines Protection Board for a handful of months, but that was long enough to have learned that a day like this would never be easy.

His partner, an older man with a heart anaesthetised by years' more experience, rolled his eyes.

"For God's sake, man," the partner spat in disgust. "It's for their own good. Now let's get this done."

They had slowed their approach to as much of a crawl as the dust-bowl road's corrugations would allow, having learned the rising orange swirl from an approaching vehicle would send the natives and their grubby little urchins scurrying like cockroaches off into the bush to avoid detection.

There had been no such warning today, but then the camp at Mimili had not often come across the radar of the protection board so the blacks weren't as skittish as elsewhere. Seemed this mob wasn't causing that much trouble.

"They should all be taken away," said his partner. "All no good, if you ask me."

He hadn't asked, as a matter of fact, but the spiel was the same every time they drew the car to a stop at a native camp.

"Look at 'em!" the older man would sneer. "Half-naked, filthy little buggers they are. Can't speak English. Useless. Never amount to anything. We're the only chance they've got. We're doing them a favour."

The younger man wasn't so sure.

Still, as patrol officers they had been charged with upholding the law of the day by visiting all the stations and settlements and camps in search of native children, half-castes mainly, who according to that same law needed protection for their own welfare.

And that had brought the men here to Mimili in the north of South Australia, or more precisely to Everard Park, the cattle station where the blacks were squatting for the time being. They tended to just up and move along whenever they felt like it, which was part of the reason the children needed protection. A nomadic lifestyle was no place for a kid. Particularly in this country.

The younger officer knew this was what the law said, and still the thought of taking the youngsters from their mothers turned his stomach. He couldn't help it. He would never get used to that keening and wailing from the mothers. At least, the father in him hoped he never would.

With a final swallow, he pushed open the car door and stepped out into the blaze of afternoon sunshine.

There didn't seem to be any men around. Just the women and children. Good. That would make things a little easier.

The women, seated around the camp, stared suspiciously as the two men stepped from the car. Clearly from the government. Clearly not to be trusted. But they felt no real fear and made no move to rise from their cross-legged position in the shade of their wiltjas (shelters).

From the corner of his eye, the younger man spotted three small girls — just babies, really — standing shyly a few feet from the car, silent and curious. They wore matching floral dresses, the colours of the fabric striking against their smooth caramel-coloured young skin. Sisters. Half-castes.

His partner had seen them too, and the hint of a sinister smile twitched at the corner of the older man's mouth. He nodded almost imperceptibly in the direction of the children to make sure his namby-pamby young partner knew precisely what was about to happen, and moved gently forward, holding out a hessian bag for the girls' inspection.

"Look," he cooed. "I have a present for you!"

The children inched closer to the man's outstretched arm. He reached into the bag and, edging closer with each word, brought forth two shining pieces of fruit.

"See? Apples and oranges! You want them? They're for you…"

The girls' eyes widened and, smiling in anticipation, they stepped closer to inspect the gift.

"They're all…for…you…apples and oranges…"

The man leaned closer and closer until the three pairs of little brown arms reached for their prize.

"NOW!" he barked, and the younger man leapt forward, bringing his arms around behind the tiny forms of the startled children and sending the incongruously glossy pieces of fruit flying into the red dust.

The sudden movement brought the women to their feet, screaming with shock and fear at the swift realisation of what was happening.

It took just seconds to lift the confused girls into the car's cavernous back seat. The women's fists rained anguished but futile blows against the officers' backs and their shrieking pleas went similarly unheeded as the doors of the car slammed shut on a world the three children would never again know as home.

The young man glanced in the rear-vision mirror as he drove away, pressing his foot as hard as he dared on the accelerator as the car lurched in time with his emotions.

"It's okay, it's okay, it's okay, it's okay," he chanted, as much in an effort to still his own pounding heart as to soothe the frightened children.

Behind them, swallowed in a cloud of dust and heart-splitting fear, the mothers' feet pounded the red dirt tracks in desperate but fruitless pursuit of the car that was spiriting their tjitjis away.

The wretched women grew smaller in the mirror, but it would take much longer for their tortured faces and grief-stricken keening to recede from the young welfare officer's memory.

"It's okay, it's okay, it's okay…"

It would be, wouldn't it? It was for their own good, wasn't it? Wasn't it?

• • • •

Reggie:

I remember my younger sister Daisy and the others being taken away. She was taken to Quorn. Lots of children were taken, even taken from the breast. Babies that were still being breast-fed were taken.

They came and offered tjitji things from a big bag. They had a bag with apples and oranges and when the kids went to get the fruit, they grabbed them. I ran away. I was frightened. I was really scared – I knew something was wrong. Now I realise it was a bribe.

I was hiding in the bush and they took the little kids away. My brothers and I ran away and hid. We raced away from that place. It wasn't just mixed-race children they were taking, they were taking the Aboriginal children too.

Mum didn't know what was happening. She didn't know what to do. I remember my mother being devastated. She was crying and sobbing and making this wailing noise and holding her head in her hands. Her heart broke. My mother and father kept asking questions about what happened to Daisy, but they couldn't get any answers.

We didn't know what had happened. We'd run away so we didn't actually see the car take Daisy and the other kids away. Three of them were taken – Daisy, Muriel and Eileen.

Everyone was crying when they were taken away. They didn't know where Daisy went. Everybody crying, couldn't find her. No-one would tell them where she was. We think they took her to Oodnadatta first.

Three were taken; two came back after they finished school, I think in the '70s. Muriel told her story in a book. Yami (Lester – who is brother, Anangu way, to Reggie) was taken away but that was to go to school in Adelaide. He came back eventually.

Muriel was one of the children taken away from the Uluru family at Mimili that day. She was just five years old when she was taken to Colebrook Children's Home in Quorn, nearly 1000km away. Her mother was Munyi, a Yankunytjatjara woman (also mother to Cassidy Uluru) and her biological father was English, but had she not been snatched that day, it was her step-father Paddy Uluru who would have "grown her up" as he did her brothers Reggie, Andrew and Cassidy.

Muriel went on to become a nurse, marry a Swedish man named Olsson and have four children of her own. Her recollections are included in a collection of accounts by Aboriginal contributors called Women of the Centre[1], an excerpt from which tells of the devastating impact of being taken away from her family at that tender age:

> *I saw my mother in 1968 – first time since 1936. We just stood and couldn't understand a word. It was the cruellest thing. I don't know if I would have been brave enough if I'd know it was going to be like that, if I'd know it was going to cut so deep, but I'm really glad I did for the sake of (my) kids because they really love their family up there.*
>
> *I think probably a lot of Aboriginal people have been made to feel ashamed of what they are. That's another really traumatic thing you had to cope with when you grew up, that you wanted to go back to your own but you didn't sort of know how to go about it without the language and with that feeling also that you didn't quite know what to expect because of the kinds of things you'd been fed on. Wondering also how your relatives would feel and receive you.*

Muriel also gave evidence to the Bringing Them Home[2] enquiry, recounting the swift suppression of language among children separated from their families:

It was forbidden for us to talk in our own language. If we had been able, we would have retained it…we weren't allowed to talk about anything that belonged to our tribal life.

The five-year-old child who reached for those apples and oranges that day became a woman who was eventually able to forgive, if never forget:

You can't live with hatred and hurting eating you out or bitterness of any kind. That's just my experience of life. Unless you get rid of that bitterness and hatred and whatever that's bugging you, you can only be half a person, not the person you should be, could be.

• • • •

As with much of the Uluru story, it is difficult to piece together the precise details of the puzzle surrounding the forced removal of family members as children, but the wounds clearly still cut deep, as they do for so many families of the thousands of children taken by paradoxically titled welfare and protection agencies over the six decades between 1910 and 1970*.

The story of how Daisy, Muriel and Eileen were snatched from the bosom of their Uluru family, although told here with some creative license, is by no means unusual. Many of the recollections from those who were and are part of what we now know as the Stolen Generation tell remarkably similar tales of deception and trickery, and of the generations-long devastation wrought by whitefella policies masquerading as "welfare and protection" measures.

Some tell of children being unceremoniously herded like sheep into the backs of trucks and spirited away from their families; of babies being ripped literally from the breast of their mothers and placed in wooden crates for transport; of being lured away with sweets or adventures or told they were going on a picnic, never to return; of being hauled away on camels, on horseback, on trains and in cars and taken hundreds, sometimes thousands, of miles away from their country, some never to return.

Parents tell of futile life-long searches for their lost children and children recall being told their parents were dead; of being forbidden to speak their native language and of never knowing of their Aboriginal heritage.

Authorities at times targeted half-caste children, but often happily swept full-blood youngsters up in the catch of the day. Anecdotal evidence suggests that children who didn't have surnames would be taken, as if this was some kind of indication of neglect. Perhaps this in part accounts for why Anangu often asked for their children to be given the whitefella surnames of station owners or missionaries.

Parents and families were seldom told of either the reasons for the forced removal of their children or their whereabouts, and those who were told were sometimes cajoled into accepting that their children had been removed for their own good. And sometimes, sadly, that was the case.

It must be said that not all removals were forced, and that not all those who were taken from their families had brutal experiences at the hands of authorities, but many were and many did. And almost all resulted in generational trauma through loss of language, culture and, ultimately, identity. Even those identified as members of the Stolen Generation who recall their experiences after removal as mostly positive express deep regret at the loss of a sense of belonging.

Sammy Wilson (nephew to Reggie and Cassidy and grandson of Paddy) was a child of mixed race and was himself at times on the radar of authorities but was saved from removal by family members on various occasions. Sammy – who, as Paddy's eldest grandson is nominal "head" of the family – is acutely aware of the dreadful and generations-long impact of forced removal on his family and on Anangu society as a whole.

Sammy:

The stolen generation made it very difficult for making sure of right way marriage. Already that has happened. Someone might be stolen from this community and someone might be stolen from that community and they end up they don't know where they're from. They might get together and they are wrong way – they marry and then they come back and everyone says, "Hey – you are wrong way! You can't marry!" A grindstone with two sides to it – that's what they might say about you if you marry wrong way.

They were taken away and told not to speak their own language.

When we would see them again, we could see clearly that they were Anangu but they spoke English. They didn't speak their own language. We couldn't speak to them. We would think, "You've grown up with white people and speaking English – you're not like my family anymore." It really broke families apart.

Because they grew up with English and speaking English and with whitefella ways it wasn't really possible for them to come back. It would have been really good if they could have come back and talked up about their father and mother and gone into Parliament and talked up about how terrible that act of taking children away was – particularly because they were part of this custodian group of Uluru.

Our concern in this forum is for the experience of the Uluru family, but there is much for the student of history to investigate in terms of the policies, and their timelines, that resulted in the undeniably painful chapter of Australia's story that we have come to call the Stolen Generation. There is a similarly vast range of personal and first-hand accounts that document the lasting trauma of those policies, but even the briefest of overviews serves to give a glimpse into the motivation – well intentioned and otherwise – of those times.

From 1908, the South Australian Children's Act allowed for the removal of Aboriginal children from their families if they were deemed neglected or destitute. (Mimili and much of the Uluru family's ancestral country lies within the whitefella-drawn boundaries of that state, although the policies and laws of the Northern Territory follow a similar pattern.) Criteria for such a judgement was stacked markedly against Anangu tribal life:

> *"…if he or she sleeps in the open air and does not satisfy the justices that he or she has a home or a settled place of abode (and if) he or she has no sufficient means of subsistence…and whose relations are…in indigent circumstances and unable to support a child".*

It is easy to see how this definition of neglect and destitution could be applied to the children of a largely nomadic tribal group such as were the Uluru family or, as the Bringing Them Home report notes, "if parents were involved in seasonal (and therefore necessarily shifting) work or impoverished through the loss of their land".

The appointed "protector" of Aborigines at the time, believed that all children of mixed-race should be deemed neglected and argued successfully that the requirement for court hearings be scrapped because the courts sometimes refused to agree with the assessment that children were neglected or destitute. The Aborigines Act of 1911 gave the Chief Protector legal guardianship of every Aboriginal and "half-caste" child, and wholesale removal began in earnest.

In this "protector's" opinion, "children should be committed to the care of (the state) where they will be educated and trained to useful trades and occupations and prevented from acquiring the habits and customs of the Aborigines, and I feel sure that they will as a rule grow up useful, self-supporting members of the community instead of developing into worse than useless dependants".

A 1913 Royal Commission into the treatment of Aboriginal people sought not to address the ethics and morality of forcibly removing children from their families, but to establish the best age at which to do so. One who gave evidence, a University of Adelaide Professor, told the commission the best age for removal was about two years:

> *"The more of those half-caste children you can take away from their parents and place under the care of the state the better … when they are a*

couple of years of age they do not require so much attention and they are young enough to be attractive. I am quite aware that you are depriving the mothers of their children, and the mothers are very fond of their children; but I think it must be the rising generation who have to be considered. They are the people who are going to live on." [4]

Protection, as a policy, continued in one form or another until 1939, when the arguably more well-intentioned but ultimately even more generationally traumatic strategy of assimilation began, first as a philosophy and later, in 1951, as a policy enshrined in law. According to the Bringing Them Home report:

"It took the form of dispersal, moving people off the reserves where they had lived regulated lives to cities and towns. Dispersal had high social costs. Indigenous people who moved from the reserves found themselves financially struggling, isolated and discriminated against. Families found every aspect of their lives monitored and assessed against non-Indigenous standards that discriminated against them."

Then came welfare, a similarly destructive development in the history of Anangu according to some of the older generation of the Uluru family. The Aboriginal Affairs Act of 1962 repealed the previous blanket guardianship of all indigenous children, favouring instead the placement of Aboriginal children (who were still being removed because of neglect or poverty, real or perceived) into institutions that would aim for "the development of a positive Aboriginal identity" but the placement of children with Aboriginal families would not begin as a policy until 1967. In 1972, the Community Welfare Act did away with legislation dealing specifically with the welfare of indigenous people, and a year later the Federal Government took responsibility for Aboriginal affairs while the states retained responsibility for providing welfare to indigenous people.

Regardless of the timelines, regardless of the machinations and intricacies of government and legislation, regardless of the rights or wrongs of the prevailing attitudes of the times, regardless of the subsequent efforts of many to heal the wounds, the fractures remain.

Like many others, those three little girls snatched from the Uluru family at Mimili in 1936 eventually found their way back, but it was to a family with whom they shared blood but not kinship, not language, not culture, not identity.

Like grindstones with two sides.

Like apples and oranges.

• • • •

The Bringing Them Home report, delivered to the Australian parliament in May 1997, estimated that between 10-33 per cent of all indigenous children were separated from their families between 1910-1970.

1. From the Heart – contribution by Muriel Olsson to Women of the Centre, edited by Adele Pring, Penguin Books, 1990

2. Bringing Them Home – National inquiry into the forced separation of Aboriginal and Torres Strait Islander children from their families; 1997 – bth.humanrights.gov. au

3. Chief Protector Senior Constable WG South and University of Adelaide Professor Stirling, as quoted in "Survival in our own land: Aboriginal experiences in South Australia since 1836", Mattingley & Hampton, Sydney: Hodder & Stoughton, 1992.

4. SA Government interim submission to the Bringing Them Home report.

CHAPTER 5

"The strength from the rock"

"Uwa," says Cassidy Uluru, bending his wiry frame to kneel beside the grave. "My father, here."

The cemetery, a small patch of red-fringed earth nestled a discreet distance from the Mutitjulu community in the shadow of the ancient rock, is ringed with practical chain-mesh like a reminder of so many fences past.

On an unusually yet appropriately overcast day, Cassidy has asked to visit the place where the remains of his father Paddy and brother Andrew lie. He doesn't come here often. He doesn't usually feel the need. He keeps the spirits and memories of his loved ones inside him but today, perhaps because he has whitefella guests, he wants to show us their graves. It's the whitefella way to recognise the dead, after all.

He pushes the gate back against the small wall of red dirt and grass collected against it and steps, at first with purpose, into the cemetery. As he walks between the graves, an eclectic mix of simple crosses and elaborate headstones, his pace slows and he seems confused as he peers at one after another inscription.

With awkward dismay, we realise he can't read the English words, so we close the subtle distance we've been keeping to help him find the graves he seeks.

And there, in a perversely modest tribute to a man of such presence and lasting power, are the words we've been looking for:

"Paddy Uluru – born circa 1898 – died 18 January, 1979"

As with much of Anangu life over the past century, the concrete slab has been whitewashed but its once stark façade is gradually being reclaimed by the red soil that has pumped through the veins of this country and its inhabitants since the dawn of time.

The flowers are faded but neither the memory nor the influence of the man in whose honour they were placed.

Cassidy points to a humble and unmarked mound of ageing red earth nestled alongside his father's grave.

"My brother, there."

He turns his eyes up towards the immense face of Uluru, its hue a deep blood red in the gloomy afternoon, and the sadness behind Cassidy's gappy smile is heart-breaking. This is a man who bears so much loss. Not only the people he has loved and lost, but the past they represent and the future they will neither see nor would welcome nor understand.

• • • •

I was born in 1952 at Wallatinna Station in South Australia. Born on country, Yankunytjatjara country. Ngintaka (perentie lizard) is my Tjukurpa.* I have always been known as Cassidy Uluru; maybe I had another name when I was young but I don't remember it.**

My father (Paddy) married my mother (Munyi) at Everard Park Station, where Mimili is today. There is important story line through all that country for the Uluru family (see map on p122). I remember coming from that way back to my homeland at Uluru with my family when I was a child, but I can't remember much else.

My mum was mostly sitting with the other women and I was away from her. When I was a tjitji, I walked with my family from Mimili to Granite Downs – Mimili is the country that holds a lot of the Tjukurpa for Anangu.

I came back here with my brothers and sister. My father brought us back on a camel and walking, from Mimili. When we were travelling through Ernabella, my father's camel went lame so we changed it for the camel you can see in the picture (of the family's return to Uluru). That camel belonged to Windlass. Windlass said, "Hey, you took my camel!" but my father said, "Wiya, your camel is better for travel. My camel is good for staying in camp!" I remember when we came back

Cassidy Uluru visits the grave of his father, Paddy Uluru, at Mutitjulu cemetery.
Photo: Jen Cowley 2016

to Uluru, I didn't have trousers. I just wore a man's jacket. I'd never been to school.

I had no idea what was happening when we came back to Uluru, I was just a kid. I didn't know what to think. I didn't know what the rock was. I was kakulyaranu (shocked, awed) and I went like this (making motion of gasping and staring open-mouthed). This was the first time my father had been back to Uluru since being away after his brother was shot.

When we came back there were not many Aboriginal people here at Uluru. We camped near Mutitjulu and when my dad passed away, he was buried there where we had camped.

That became the cemetery.

When I was little, I was kicked out of the tourist area at Uluru. They didn't want me playing around where the tourists were. That used to happen quite a bit.

I became a man at Indulkana, north of Wallatinna near Granite Downs, a place called Iwantja. After my mum and dad grew me up and I was a young fella, I went to work on the cattle station, Everard Park, at Mimili.

One time, back when I was a stockman, I went to the Mount Isa rodeo. I didn't ride in the rodeo – I'm smart! I just watched.

I fell off a windmill once but I'm still alive! I was strong then. I climbed up a windmill in the middle of the night, I think it was about midnight. I don't remember why I climbed the windmill. I was a bit silly, maybe? But I fell asleep and then I fell off.

I hurt everything when I fell off. When someone came and found me, they took me back to the station homestead at Everard Park and they radioed the (Royal) Flying Doctor (Service) and they took me in that aeroplane to hospital in Alice Springs. I was half dead. Lucky we'd already learned to wear clothes by then, otherwise I would have been naked when I fell off!

I don't know how long I was in hospital. I was there a while, I think.

Alice Springs was only a small town then so it was only a small clinic. After I got better, I went back to Everard Park.

After I was a stockman, I became an Eagle Ranger (Northern Territory Conservation Commission) here at Uluru. I was looking at tourists looking at me! I drove the ranger car around looking out for everyone.

I was a good stockman. I was strong then, but not so strong now.

These days, Cassidy is a man of few words but those who know him well describe a man with a quick wit, a cheeky but respectful manner and a profound love for and connection with country and culture.

One young Aboriginal female ranger whom Cassidy mentored, and to whom he remains close, recalls him as an effective but gentle teacher:

> Cassidy is very witty, very sharp and he has an immense grasp of his own culture and what's sensitive and where the lines are for him. That family (Uluru) holds a lot of very special and deeply sacred information as a family group. They are very important people.
>
> The best times I spent with Cassidy was when he was teaching me. He taught me things I wouldn't know unless he was prepared to guide me through; information I would not have learned otherwise. He never told me anything he shouldn't have – never – but he taught me about context and why I couldn't know certain things. That's a big privilege.
>
> He always handled every question (from tourists) with grace. He never made anyone feel stupid, no matter the question.
>
> My relationship with Cassidy was a very serious one because he was a man. He was always very proper; serious but he taught everything with good humour so people felt comfortable.
>
> He thinks on a different level than other people. He understands on a different level, particularly about different cultures.[1]

Cassidy is also a man of deep spirituality and is widely regarded by those in and close to the Uluru family as having been born with the instincts and insights of a ngangkari, a traditional healer.

As his daughter, Emmy Simpson, says:

> He is very conscious of that spiritual side of things. He

has that ngangkari quality. He knew in his heart that he had that healing way. You are born a ngangkari, and it stays with you – that's Cassidy.

There's an intensity to Cassidy Uluru that is both fascinating and at times unnerving. During one conversation, he fixed me with gaze of such sudden seriousness, I feared I may have inadvertently overstepped some ephemeral cultural mark. Instead he tapped his side, just below his ribs and said: "My father sees you. He is looking at you."

According to Emmy, Cassidy often speaks of his father. "He misses the old days," she says. And it's clear from our yarns with the younger Uluru brother that he feels deeply the power of Uluru and, through it, the strength of his father Paddy.

> My father was a strong man. I think he was strong like the rock.
>
> If you watch me, you'll see the power as well – the strength from Uluru. My father gave me everything. When I sleep, I see him. He comes to me when I sleep.
>
> My dad started the fight for Uluru. We are still fighting, me and my brother Reggie. But we are getting old. It's a young fella's fight. I am happy with what Sammy is doing.

For all his and other's recollections, no story about this complex Uluru elder would be remotely complete – and neither would the man himself – without mention of the epic love story that is Tiku and Cassidy's.

It's said that Cassidy moved to Mutitjulu for his love, having met Tiku Captain there when he came up from Mimili with his brothers for a land rights meeting in the 1970s. Some recall the young and strong-willed Tiku falling almost instantly for the "flash young cowboy in the hat" and the feeling it seems was mutual from the very start, although Cassidy is quick to point out that they did not get married after the first date: "Wiya, not married straight away. We got

Cassidy Uluru 2016. *Photo: Steve Cowley*

married after we had been talking and working together for a while. We were married the Anangu way – a bush marriage."

Tiku, who was a Pitjantjatjara woman, already had two children, Emmy and Simon, and Cassidy speaks proudly of how he "grew them up". Emmy remains true to the only father she has ever known and has fond recollections to share:

I am Cassidy Uluru's step daughter in the whitefella way but I've always thought of myself as his daughter. He's always called me unta, pronounced "oon-da" and meaning daughter.

He used to tell me stories about spending time with me as a kid. He was very proud of the way I could go out in the bush and hunt lizards and that sort of thing.

He would say to me, "Alatji!" – this is how you do it. He would teach me things and show me things and so would my mother.

I've never known a time when he wasn't in my life. I always thought he was my (biological) father. I knew I had a white father, but Cassidy was a good man in my life. He's always thought of me as his own because he's never had kids of his own. He thinks of my kids as his grandkids. And the kids love him. He taught them things too. Cassidy helped to teach me right way and wrong way.

We used to live on the cemetery side of Mutitjulu when I was little, when Cassidy and Mum were working as rangers. We used to walk into Mutitjulu all the time. They were great times.

He loves his Slim Dusty. He used to play the tapes over and over in the ranger's vehicles. We'd do tours out on the back roads and it was always Slim Dusty on a loop. We'd listen to one side then we'd turn the tape over and listen to the other side, then it would start again. I grew up knowing every word to every Slim Dusty song.

Cassidy really enjoyed spending time with tourists and sharing some of his knowledge. He was pretty cheeky sometimes but always respectful with the mingas. He'd have a laugh. I remember him telling me that this tourist came up to him and said, "Is it going to rain?" and Cassidy said "Dunno – I'm not a rain God."

He and Mum were always happy to share their culture and to teach other people and it meant a lot to Cassidy to get the land back. The handback of Uluru was a very important thing for him.

Emmy misses her mother deeply, but the loss of Tiku was for Cassidy nothing short of catastrophic and the depth of his grief is still visible in many ways. The fondness with which he speaks of his wife is touching. As with his father, he keeps Tiku's spirit and memory close, and tells me with that same intensity: "My wife, Tiku, she is here looking at you too. Tiku loved me."

The pair were often separated while Cassidy continued to work as a stockman at Mimili, but the distance was only ever geographical according to Emmy:

> They were always singing each other – he would cry for her and pine for her and she would somehow just turn up. Then she'd be pining and crying for him, and he would turn up. Each would sing the other and they always just seemed to find each other.
>
> When they were older, they would still sing each other but Tiku used to pretend she wasn't singing him if she was cranky with him. He'd be away and then he'd just suddenly turn up at the door and I'd say to her, "You been singing him?" and she'd say, "Wiya – I don't want to see him!" but I knew she'd been singing him. They just had this very deep spiritual connection.
>
> She and Cassidy were a good team. They did Anangu Tours together, they were rangers together. A lot of people all around the world had photos of them, and they would send the photos back for them. They were very proud of their culture and their history. They both had great knowledge about Uluru.

Tiku was only fifty-eight when she died in 2008 from renal failure. Many hearts were broken by the loss, but none more so than Cassidy's. Those who know him well say he lost a great deal of his strength and that his heart was irreparably broken by Tiku's death. Emmy explains:

> Cassidy moved here to Alice Springs to be near Mum when she was in her final stages of renal failure.
>
> I remember him knocking on the door just after midnight one night in a panic saying Tiku couldn't breathe. We raced her to the hospital and he was sitting in the back of the car crying and moaning, "Tiku, Tiku!"
>
> He stayed with her all the way through to the end. That was heartbreaking for him. For all of us, but particularly for him.
>
> When Mum died there was a big sorry business at both Mutitjulu and at Kaltukatjara (Docker River). The funeral was at Docker River. A friend of the family helped organise the funeral and she bought all new clothes for the men – Cassidy and Reggie and all of them – but Cassidy refused to wear the new clothes. He wanted to stay in the clothes he was wearing when he was with her. He cut his hair, which is a traditional form of grieving, and he wouldn't change his clothes.
>
> Cassidy wanted Tiku to be buried at Mutitjulu, but she had always wanted to be buried at Docker River with her father (Captain No.1). That was a really sad time for us all because I felt I had to honour her wishes and it was difficult.
>
> The community was pretty upset with me because they felt Tiku and Cassidy should always be together and they wanted her to be buried at Mutitjulu but I knew I had to honour her wishes. It's about country. Docker River is her country; Mutitjulu is Cassidy's country.
>
> She told me once, when we were at Docker River, that this is where she wanted to be after she died. She'd go to the cemetery and she'd point to the graves of my grandfathers, and say "This is Captain No.1, this is Captain No.2 and this

is me..."

Cassidy lost his soul mate when Tiku died. He was completely gutted. He felt very alone.

After the funeral he moved back to the house just outside Yulara, which was the place the Department of Conservation gave them in gratitude for all Mum and Cassidy had done for them. He didn't want to leave that house and he still lives there. That's where he feels closest to Tiku. But he was just lost in his grief for the first couple of years after she died. He went to Port Augusta for two years and we didn't hear from him.

He says he can still feel her. He points to his side and says, "She is here – Tiku is here."

It's like a beautiful love story. I never knew them without each other.

They were very protective of each other. Tiku was a really beautiful lady and I miss her, but she and Cassidy, they were true loves.

• • • •

*Cassidy was born at a site that is deeply significant to the creation story of the perentie lizard man who stole a sacred grindstone. The perentie lizard man pretended to have injured his foot so he could avoid going on a hunt, thereby having the opportunity to run away with the sacred grindstone. Cassidy's birthplace is the site at which this deception took place.

**Reggie Uluru recalls that it was his brother Cassidy's mother, Munyi (Paddy Uluru's third wife) who gave him his name. Usually it is the grandfather who bestows an Anangu name. There does not seem to be any record of Cassidy having a traditional name.

1. Interview at Mutitjulu (October 2017) with Kate Vickers, a ranger with Uluru-Kata Tjuta National Parks who worked with the Uluru family and Anangu Tours. Her insights are reproduced with permission.

CHAPTER 6

"This world is not my home"

Of all the facets of indigenous cultural life, it is arguably the subject of death and dying and the associated traditional practices that hold some of the greatest fascinations for interested observers. Maybe it's the universality of that shared experience that lends it such mystique. As devotion to mainstream faiths wanes, perhaps this curiosity is borne of a quest for something to replace the comfort of religious belief when faced with life's inevitable losses.

But for Anangu, and for the Uluru family, who have collectively and individually suffered such monumental loss over the past two hundred-odd years, the subject of death is still one of the most sensitive and therefore most difficult about which to elicit insight.

This challenge is compounded by the earlier explanation of the fact that Anangu do not routinely discuss feelings as such, as whitefellas do. Anangu don't talk about feelings, they simply feel. In responding and relating to each other, they don't need to ask the default whitefella "How do you feel?" question. They understand and know each other on a visceral level that makes the question unnecessary.

The reluctance to mention the names of the dead is common to most Australian indigenous cultures, and so it is for Anangu who instead use the generic term "Kunmanara" to replace the name of the deceased, and there are deeply sacred traditions and rituals around death that are not discussed beyond those to whom that knowledge belongs.

These are cultural considerations that complicate the gathering of information for a family story but such is their acceptance of the need to foster greater understanding, the Uluru elders were patient and kind in their approach to my curiosity, offering as much insight as possible while remaining true to Tjukurpa.

I share this insight here, and elsewhere throughout this story, with their blessing and with respect and acknowledgement that the discussion of the dead and the repeating of their names may cause discomfort for some Anangu.

During a visit to Docker River in 2015, I spent some memorable time out on country with a group of Anangu women and asked them, amongst other things, what they do when someone dies. My question was met with confused surprise:

"Well, we're Lutheran," they told me. "We have a funeral, of course."

After rephrasing the question, the women told of some of the traditional practices around death, but their initial response was a reminder of the enormous and lasting influence of Christian missionaries over Anangu society and culture.

In later discussions about the deaths of family members, including Paddy Uluru and Tiku (Cassidy's wife), again the juxtaposition of the two faiths – Christianity and Tjukurpa – came into sharp focus but while the process around actual interment is largely based on mainstream religious practice, Tjukurpa is in no way diminished by it. The spiritual connection to the dead, their country, their family and their storyline remains undimmed and is, for the moment at least, the greater comfort to Anangu.

Community elder:

Paddy was an old man when he died*. They looked after him at the clinic in Mutitjulu. They gave him some tablets but they told us he didn't have much time left. They were camped out at Paddy's camp. He just went to sleep. There wasn't any money for a coffin or a funeral or anything. People didn't have any money for coffins in those days so they would use sheets. They would use boxes, not proper coffins just boxes. That was before the Lands Council days, when they set up a kind of funeral fund. (Paddy) was wrapped in a sheet and the rangers helped to dig the hole to put him in. He was laid to rest in a white sheet. An Aboriginal pastor from King's Canyon side, a man named Peter Bulla, was camping here and he prayed for the funeral ceremony. Big mob from Mimili came. Family came from everywhere – Alice Springs and everywhere. It was a very nice ceremony and Paddy's grave became the first in that cemetery; that's why the cemetery is there. After that, many of the people who were buried in that cemetery were visitors who just happened to be here when they passed away.[**]

There is no doubt that with Paddy being such a luminary figure in Anangu society, traditional mourning rituals would have been part of the grieving process for community and for his extended family. There would have been a lengthy sorry business[***] for the "big mob" of mourners to which the Mutitjulu elder refers, but the traditional bereavement ceremonies and customs that accompanied the grieving for the father of the Uluru family are not for public consumption.

Tiku's death was similarly mourned widely by the communities of Mutitjulu and Docker River, and many others besides, and it is a privilege to have been given a little culturally appropriate insight into how her loss was mourned in both the Christian and Tjukurpa traditions.

One who spoke of the funeral recalled the Christian service as a deeply emotional and desperately sad occasion to which "many, many, many people came to mourn the loss of someone who was such a big part of this world". However, rather than adhering to the often stiff-upper lipped and emotionally sparse constraints of western-style Christian grieving, those who mourned Tiku's death gave voice to their anguish in the traditional Anangu way:

> The family all came together and they sat down and wailed. It's a lovely but very intense thing to hear. It's a raw, honest outpouring of grief. There's no hiding the emotion or tapering it off to fit with western society's idea of dignified grief. It's beautiful. It's a sound you don't forget, the sound of absolute loss. The sound of the ripping away of a huge part of someone. They are unashamed to show that hurt and pain

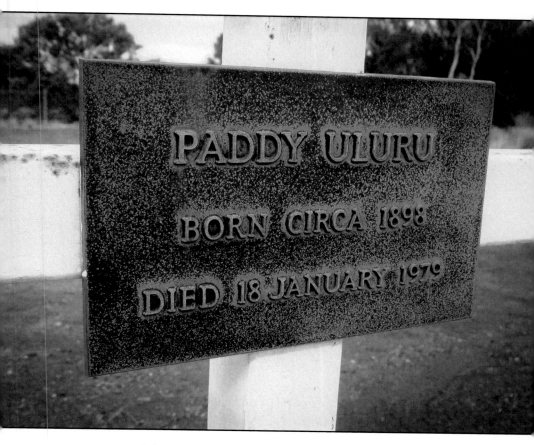

A simple plaque for a remarkable man. *Photo: Jen Cowley*

for the loss of someone so important.

There was a lot of stuff that happened in sorry camp, particularly with the older women, that I can't talk about or tell you about. Lots of traditional stuff. But in general, when someone dies, the family will sweep the houses. From my superficial understanding, they get a certain branch from a certain tree and use it to sweep not only the house, but the car or wherever that person was in life. The whole family will sweep the premises and those objects to cleanse that space and let that space settle again so as not have those negative feelings.

Kunmanara is the word you use in place of the name of someone who has died. Same goes for someone who has the same name as the person who has died – you'll refer to that person (who is still alive) as Kunmanara – that person won't have their name pronounced until such time as the family deems it appropriate to use it again. That is entirely up to the family. I've known people who have only ever been called Kunmanara in all my years here.****

I think it's a good way within Anangu culture that they take time with their grief. Changes in life, your age, your children, getting grey hair – these are the points that are marked as celebrations, as milestones. Life events are not rushed. For Anangu dealing with death, it's about the whole family sitting down and marking that pain, then recognising when it's the time for that pain to pass and then the time for the family to go back to get on with their lives while never forgetting the person they loved and lost.[1]

The unfettered expression of emotion and grief is not the only traditional aspect of Anangu mourning that is vulnerable to the incursion of Christianity. Also susceptible to dilution are those sacred rituals and beliefs surrounding death but, true to Tjukurpa and in keeping with the remarkable resilience of these people, Anangu have been able to blend the old with the new in a fusion that goes at least some of the way to satisfying both faiths. Not that this compromise comes without challenge, as I discovered through a long, unforgettable and educative discussion with extended Uluru family member Alan Wilson (father to Sammy, Anangu way) one warm March afternoon around a campfire:

Before we knew about Christianity, in traditional times, (the bodies of deceased) people were placed in a hollow and covered by branches. Then the soul, the spirit, stays there. Then after people have done their grieving – after a certain period, maybe one year, maybe two years – they all gather together and come back to that burial place. Before they arrive at the gravesite, two ngangkari (traditional healer) will go on ahead and one will do some ceremony.

These days they cement a grave but in the old days they would put a stick or some kind of marker on the grave and the spirit would stay and wait on the top of that marker. The spirit is crying. Then the ngangkari gets the spirit off that marker and puts it inside himself, here on his chest, and then the family comes.

They call out as they come from the sorry camp and the calls are answered. They come and they all sit down and wail and cry and grieve again and they cover themselves with the earth. The ngangkari has already retrieved the spirit. He asks the widow to sit down and he goes to her and places the spirit inside her so they are then together forever.

That spirit then, especially at night, will keep you safe. If there's danger approaching or something bad is about to happen, that spirit will warn you and keep you safe. That spirit keeps an eye out and alerts you: "Watch out! There is danger." Someone comes along with a gun and you have nothing, that spirit will stop the bullet. Without that spirit, they will shoot you. The spirit blocks him. Something will happen to that person's gun and they will not be able to fire and you will not be shot. That spirit protects you.

Nowadays we take people to the cemetery. What happens to their spirit? Buggered things up. Wrong way. That box – that coffin – it traps the spirit. The spirit can't get out and the Ngangkari can't put that spirit into the loved ones, so they are unprotected. That spirit can't protect them. That's because it's trapped in that coffin.

There are also some long held and widespread misconceptions about dying and death in the piranpa world – misunderstandings, borne from a nucleus of truth, that give rise to continuing suspicion and fear of whitefella practices. The notion of autopsy has been wrongly extrapolated into the belief that whitefellas always cut bodies up so they can fit into coffins and the practice of organ donation has been similarly misconstrued as the automatic removal of all the dead person's organs which are then arbitrarily given away. Similar misunderstanding of blood transfusions has given rise to the notion that blood is extracted from dead people for use in medical procedures.

After explaining the processes of autopsy, organ donation and blood transfusions, our companions seemed a little more at ease but their scepticism and alarm is understandable. To Anangu, these practices would irreparably disturb the way things are meant to be – that is that the deceased person's body, and therefore soul or spirit, are returned whole from whence they came – to the earth, to the spirit world.

> Our way, someone dies, everyone goes to them. They sit down together and they cry. Crying is a help. You really grieve and you think about your grief and you're sharing that. Sometime after that funeral, you can carry on, you are not dwelling on it. But the person who has suffered that loss, they are the ones you make sure you are really looking after.
>
> When I finish up, when I go to sleep and I am buried under the ground, I will die with all my knowledge inside me. All my Tjukurpa. All the young people – granddaughters and grandsons – they won't have that knowledge. It will go with me because it's inside me. But other people, my own brother, my son and the ones I have raised, the ones I grew up, they will have some of that knowledge from me because I will have taught them and they will have learned some of that knowledge from me.
>
> We've been put on this earth and we were given our culture and our knowledge so that we can live well and happy, but this world is not my home. The spirit goes where their Tjukurpa is. So my Tjamu, he is out here.

To Anangu, death is only the end of the body's physical existence. The soul or the spirit, on the other hand, is indestructible. And isn't that, in essence, what we would all like to believe? Isn't that what gives us comfort? For all our cultural differences, the experience of loss and grief is one shared by all humanity.

Seldom has this truth been more profoundly apparent, to me at least, than through the kindness of these gentle Uluru family elders when, around the universally comforting glow of a campfire, I shared a story of my own grief for a lost brother.

You have just told us about your brother and it sounds like you are singing for him to be here with you. I say to you that your brother IS here with you. You are happy to be here with us in the bush, eating good food so that's good. Pukulpa, pukulpa (all right, good). And I say, as Aboriginal people, when we lose somebody we embrace and cry and then inside we get happiness. With your brother, you are bound. One mother, you are bound. Anangu understand your sorrow. That culture is strong.

This is Australia that we live in. We all live here, all of us. We are all Anangu and this country says to us that we are all part of it and we must all embrace each other and help each other grieve when we have loss. You come to this place, this beautiful place and to Aboriginal people and to their country. You share that with them and you embrace them and then you are at peace. That's how it works.

Doesn't matter where you are born or where you are from. If you are from long, long away or if you are from right here, you are Anangu. We are all people. Come and see and embrace and we are happy. When you embrace and you are sharing that grief with all your family, all your people, then you are at peace again.

The physical embrace in which I was then enfolded by these members of the Uluru family was as warm as the afternoon and the campfire's coals. It needed no translation, no cultural interpretation, no anthropological explanation. Their kindness and understanding are a reminder that for all our differences, we are all human.

•••••

* Because there are no official demographic records from the time, Paddy Uluru's exact birth date is unknown. It is estimated that he was born around 1898 and his death date is recorded as January 18, 1979. Based on these dates, Paddy would have been around 81 when he died.

** This recollection came from a community elder who is connected and close to the Uluru family but who, through devotion to Tjukurpa and the "proper way" did not wish to be mentioned by name.

*** "Sorry business" is the term widely used across Australian Aboriginal communities for the period of mourning following a death.

**** Words that resemble that of the deceased are also often replaced for the period of mourning, however long the family deems that to be, by words from a neighbouring language. Photographs of the deceased are also problematic and in official displays, such as at the Uluru-Kata Tjuta Cultural Centre, photographs are often covered if the person in the image has died. Elsewhere, as contemporary life and technology move on and the depiction of Aboriginal people is widespread, this can present great difficulty. It is not always practical or possible to remove images of the dead but often for an organisation, presentation or publication (for example on film or in a book such as this) a warning will precede the body of work to warn Aboriginal people that it may contain images of deceased people.

1. Interview at Mutitjulu (October 2017) with Kate Vickers, a ranger with Uluru-Kata Tjuta National Parks who worked with the Uluru family and Anangu Tours. Her insights are reproduced with permission.

CHAPTER 7

—

Black Mist

The day's conversation had wandered, or so it seemed to a whitefella, like a spider's web of lines, crossing and intersecting but leading back always and forever to the heart of a family and its history.

As the shadow of the great rock lengthened and tendrils of smoke from the campfire eddied up into the late afternoon's pink glow, talk turned as it had for decades around Uluru campfires, to the story of another, more malignant smoke; the story of the day the earth shook and a sinister "black mist" crept across the country.

Sitting cross-legged on the ground of their father Paddy's camp in the shadow of Uluru more than sixty years on, his sons Reggie and Cassidy, and family member Alan Wilson, recalled that day – October 15, 1953. The day the first nuclear bomb test in Central Australia was detonated.

Cassidy, who was born at Wallatinna Station in 1952, was just a year old, so his memories are those passed down through family lore, but both Reggie (who would have been a teenager at the time) and Alan (slightly younger) remember the day very clearly and described it with great animation:

> People were really strong and healthy.
>
> Then that thing arrived in our country. That bomb and the big cloud that came and it sent sickness across our country. The winds took it across the country and spread that sickness out – then everyone was sick.
>
> We were sheltering in a cave in the rocks near Mimili (Everard Park). We stayed in that cave, we didn't go out. We were too frightened to go out during the day. When the late day came and the dust settled down, my father would go out to hunt so we could have food.

We saw the explosion (the mushroom cloud). Some people, maybe the whitefellas, might have known what it was but all us bush people, we just remember this huge BOOM and then the cloud that rose up and we were just confused.

We thought, "What IS that?" We had never seen anything like it. We felt the ground shake too. The earth moved under us. We thought, well, it's something maybe not too good so let's go into that cave for shelter. All the old men and women said "Let's go and find shelter because otherwise we might die".

It might have been a long way from us, but we saw it – it was such a huge cloud of dust. It went really high up into the sky. The wind dispersed it, but it also got rid of all the people.

We didn't know what it was. Most people didn't know what it was. But those older people had an idea that it was a deadly thing. Some of the people had maybe been told that it was dangerous and that you could die so that's why we all fled and hid.

Yami Lester became blind because of it. His eyes were affected because he saw it but his eyes came good again for a while, though.

When we think, in a contemporary context, of the testing of nuclear weapons in Central Australia, it is the name Maralinga that has become synonymous with those activities but it was the testing carried out in 1953 at the Emu Field site that made the lasting impression on the Uluru family and its members, many of whom were at the time living at Wallatinna and Mimili, less than 200km from "ground zero". It was this initial test in central Australia that was deemed by the investigations of the 1984-85 Royal Commission into British Nuclear Testing in Australia to have been the likely source of the "black mist" that had become so much a part of the Anangu narrative since the mid-1950s.

At the time of the Royal Commission, headed up by Justice Jim McClelland, it was suggested that this consciousness of something called a "black mist" arose as a result of media attention, but stories of the "cloud of sickness" were nothing new to the Uluru family, or to other Anangu. It was only wider Australia that knew little of the tale until 1980 when Yami Lester – brother to Reggie and Cassidy in Anangu way – heard a radio interview in which he felt the issue of the treatment of indigenous people during the nuclear testing had been misrepresented.

"All day I thought about what (was) said (in that interview). And things started coming back to me... a lot of people listened (to that interview) and they probably thought everything was all right when he said, "Don't worry about it, boys, we took care of the blackfellas".[1]

Yami contacted a journalist he knew, hoping to tell the other side of the story. It was the resulting Adelaide Advertiser articles that essentially lit the fire of public interest which in turn prompted the government to establish a Royal Commission.

Many Anangu gave evidence to the commission, including Yami, but detractors continued to intimate that the memories were based either on mystical mumbo-jumbo or inspired by the investigation itself.

However, a number of white people also bore witness that helped to verify the Anangu testimony including Professor Annette Hamilton[2] who attested that the "black mist" as it had become known by then, had been talked about around Anangu gatherings long before media interest brought it to wider society's attention. While conducting doctorate research in central Australia in 1970-71, Professor Hamilton said she heard accounts from the people at Mimili of the event:

> "It is also worth noting that all these people would have an intimate understanding of normal physical events in their environment, and all noted that the puyu (smoke/mist) was different to anything they had previously experienced. A dust-storm might be the most comparable phenomenon, but this is always accompanied by a strong wind, whereas all those witnesses who mentioned wind described it at the time as a "breeze". Mists, which do occur rarely during the cold seasons, might be

similar in some respects but they do not usually move and are white in colour. Therefore, the description of this as a unique phenomenon has considerable credibility." (RC Report p.185)

The Royal Commission's report[3] was handed down in early 1985, coincidentally the same year of the handback of Uluru-Kata-Tjuta to the Anangu. While the findings and the commission itself were challenged (chiefly from the British government), with allegations of bias, it makes for fascinating reading and an insightful timeline of events leading up to and following the detonation of that first test bomb at Emu Field at 6.57am on October 15, 1953. Much has been written and debated in the three decades since that report and a plethora of information exists for the interested observer to pursue, but the report provides a comprehensive overview for the purpose of background for this significant chapter in the Uluru family's story.

One of the early statements in the report sounds a warning for what follows, albeit with a gentle reminder of the context of what was known at the time of testing:

> *"The radiological safety recommendations developed for Maralinga in 1955-56… were appropriate when considered in light of the international radiation protections standards of the time (but) the regulations for these and earlier tests were not always complied with." (Royal Commission's 1985 Report p.71)*

As part of its brief, the commission devoted a considerable effort to the investigation of the treatment of and impact on Aboriginal populations, communities and society of nuclear testing, and prefaced its comments by saying:

> *"From an unknown time – but certainly for long before the arrival of white people Aboriginal people had used the lands around where the tests took place. The knowledge and use of these lands provided the people with life sustenance systems which impressed some of those outsiders who first came in contact with them:*

"During the latter part of the last century, explorers travelling through the north-west of South Australia described the Pitjantjatjara and Yankunytjatjara as people suffering no obvious deprivations in an environment depressingly inhospitable to Europeans. They told of natives whose easy, ingenious adaptations to the land revealed a long-established confidence in dealing with the rigours of the desert. [Toyne and Vachon 1984, pp.21-2]."

"Aboriginal people interacted with, and often helped, these explorers who were later followed by dingo bounty hunters, missionaries and pastoralists. Traditionally, Aboriginal people moved around the lands. From both old and new, permanent and semi-permanent locations, people were constantly traversing the country. Traditionally, there were the hunting and gathering activities with groups of up to 25 men, women and children travelling through the deserts, the groups constantly forming and re-forming, splitting and re-combining. Ceremonial activities also were a reason for movement, engaging people in travel over large distances… bringing together large numbers of people, and continually re-establishing spiritual and social connections. There were also the less formal and less regular movements which people would undertake to visit their relatives and their friends.

"After contact with non-Aborigines, another pattern of movement emerged but did not displace the traditional, less permanent relocations… by the time the testing grounds were declared prohibited to their traditional owners, traditional movement patterns had been modified by changing centres of population…but the movements had not ceased to occur. The country was still used for hunting and gathering, for temporary settlements, for caretaking and spiritual renewal, and for traverse by people who moved from locations to other areas Within and outside what became the prohibited zones. The immediate areas used for the nuclear tests and those areas surrounding them were not totally uninhabited wastelands as evidence produced before the Royal Commission from Aboriginal and non-Aboriginal sources shows." (p.151-152)

The 1947 appointment of a Native Patrol Officer acknowledged that there was a general awareness of Aboriginal people still inhabiting and using the country around the site at Woomera at least, where, regardless of indigenous population, the decision had already been made to establish a long-range guided missile facility.

That officer was W.B. MacDougall, who was based at Woomera from 1949.

In his 1993 biography, Yami Lester recalls meeting MacDougall and by his account, and the impression given by reports quoted in the Royal Commission report, the patrol officer was a man of good intention.

"I was at Wallatinna and I remember that patrol officer used to come to the camp," Yami recalled. "All the Anangu called him kuta, brother. He had three fingers on his right hand, if I remember rightly, and he used to shake hands with his left. His name was Mr MacDougall."

As one man with limited resources, MacDougall's job, viewed as always with the benefit of hindsight, was almost impossible from the start, faced as he was with vast distances and an even more vast cultural divide. At first, it seemed the task would not be particularly onerous, given his early patrols to ascertain indigenous population numbers were mostly to grazing properties in the region around Woomera, and there were often railway sidings and wells that also offered easy headcounts of Aboriginal people and the opportunity give "some consideration to general Aboriginal health and welfare".

However, the patrols necessarily extended further in line with extensions to the intended LRWER (Long Range Weapons Establishment Range) Prohibited Areas, and as the distances increased, so did the difficulty in gathering accurate information about the inhabitants of the land.

In 1950, MacDougall reported that he felt he had accounted for:

> "...all aborigines south of the Central Reserve with the possible exception of a tribe reported to be occupying the sandhill country somewhere between Coober Pedy and Laverton in Western Australia."

However, in the same report he writes of the need for "an authentic census" to "protect the project from adverse criticism" and suggests:

> "…a need for a reconnaissance to determine to what extent tribal natives are occupying territory within the Central Reserve and over which the range will pass, and that plans for a reconnaissance should be made as early as possible." (p.155-6)

In early 1952 MacDougall began to patrol the Central Reserve, an area covering more than 60,000 square miles (or close to 100,000km), and again it is clear that the scope of the brief and the vastness of the region made the task at hand difficult to say the least. It was not through MacDougall's lack of trying, as the commission's report points out:

> "The objectives of the March 1952 patrol set out clearly a broad range of unknown aspects of Aboriginal demography and lifestyle which MacDougall obviously felt should be investigated if Aboriginal safety and welfare were to be guaranteed. That he was not completely successful in achieving his objectives is shown in the report written after the patrol was undertaken:
>
>> "The trip was successful in the Northern portion but only partially so in the Southern section. The information secured in regard to the Mann and Tompkinson Ranges is as accurate as possible without a personal visit to the area. Accuracy was made possible only because I have known the people concerned for a long time and (a missionary) acted as an interpreter when I was in difficulty with the language. The aborigines from the above areas were visiting Ernabella.
>>
>> "The natives of the Everard Range area (which almost certainly included members of the Uluru family at the time) have not known me for so long and they were not prepared to speak so freely of areas with secret life significance. They spoke freely of areas that had no importance to tribal life apart from

hunting grounds. It was not possible to determine the degree of importance as commonly under such circumstances they depend upon the inaccessibility of the actual sacred areas and the natural camouflage of water supplies to prevent trespassing.

"I commenced enquiries at the Musgrave Range, which is occupied by the Pitjantjatjara tribe. Owing to the gradual drift South, which I believe has been going on for hundreds of years almost imperceptibly, but has accelerated when white contacts occur, it is difficult to determine the boundaries of tribal country. I was surprised to find that there are a number of natives still living entirely upon the northern portion of the reserve in South Australia. The area over which they travel extends beyond the South Australian border into the Northern Territory and Western Australia.

"They show very little interest in those things that can only be got from the white man and visit the missions or white communities only once or twice every two or three years. I am sure that the establishment of the range up to (the) 500-mile point on the eastern side will have no detrimental results. I have had no opportunity to investigate the position on the Western side, so cannot express an opinion." (p.157)

Regardless of what MacDougall did or didn't find, the decision had already been made by authorities to investigate the desert regions of South Australia for a nuclear test site by the time of his appointment. MacDougall clearly had some inkling that history would one day scrutinise the treatment of indigenous people in the conduct of these nuclear tests, because in one of his reports to the range superintendent in 1951, he offered this advice:

"I suggest that some concrete evidence be given to the United Nations or International authorities that the rights of the Aborigines are not being disregarded, and that consideration comparable to that

shown to the white people concerned with range activities is in effective progress, e.g. range overseer activities, safety measures, compensation, and good relations." (p.162)

From his reports, the commission concluded that MacDougall did indeed believe his job was to protect Aboriginal welfare in its many forms, both within the actual rocket range area and beyond, particularly as the breadth of the range increased. Not all those in authority shared his view. The range area's superintendent made a handwritten note on the front of MacDougall's report, to the effect that the patrol officer had been interviewed and "...there is no immediate need for extension of investigations (further along) the range" (p.163)

More investigations were conducted throughout 1953 to ascertain the numbers and nature of the Aboriginal populations that lived on and used the area – specifically the country around Granite Downs, Everard Park (Mimili) and Wallatinna, which is traditional Uluru family country and Paddy and his sons and family would almost certainly have been inhabiting this region at the time, having not yet returned to Uluru from self-imposed "exile" at Mimili after the shooting of Paddy's brother at the rock in 1934.

However, it was documented in one of his reports that MacDougall, having canvassed the "natives" in the region believed "...no action is really necessary other than to avoid arousing interest in that area or making any reference to white man activity."

In August 1953 MacDougall, accompanied by another patrol officer by the name of Morrison, visited station managers across the region to warn of the coming bomb trials, and then visited other stations including at Oodnadatta, Welbourn Hill, Granite Downs, Everard Park, Wallatinna. In each case, the warning was delivered to the property manager who was then left to inform the Aboriginal people of the impending detonations. In evidence given to the commission, Morrison said that "in the case of Wallatinna, he assumed this information was passed on although he did not actually see or hear this happen".

The commission report stated that, according to evidence submitted:

> *At each place populations of people and grazing animals were recorded. In September (MacDougall) undertook a patrol to check on the location of the Yankunytjatjara people counted during his 1952 patrol.*
>
> *Despite finding that the dingo pup hunters travelled further west than he had previously thought, he reported that he had accounted for all of the people noted in his previous report.*
>
> *On the day of the Totem 1 test he confidently wrote to the Superintendent of the Range:*
>
> *"There is no fear of Jangkuntjara [sic] natives moving out of pastoral areas, nor is there any possibility of natives based on missions or stations in South Australia moving south of the reserve."*
>
> *Morrison, at least with hindsight, did not share MacDougall's confidence that all of the Aboriginal people were necessarily accounted for. While describing MacDougall as 'magnificent' and 'very sympathetic', he went on to say "In a vast area like that it would be impossible to guarantee any protection for natives. They could be sitting behind a salt bush and you would never know: even low flying aircraft would not pick them up. So, in that sense, he would be a foolish man to guarantee that he could ensure us that there were no natives in the area…" "* (p.172-73)

However, authorities took what, again in retrospect, was the incomplete and inadequate assessment of the habitation of the region and the possible impact of the testing on Aboriginal people and informed the Prime Minister of the day, Sir Robert Menzies:

> *"…we are able to assure you that the isolation of the site of the trials precludes any possible damage to habitation or living beings by the "shock" wave, thermal radiation, gamma rays and neutrons. It is possible for us to assure you that the time of firing will be chosen so that any risk to health due to radioactive contamination to our cities, or in fact of human beings, is impossible."*

The commission's assessment is damning:

> "No special consideration was given to the lifestyles of Aboriginal people (which included members of the Uluru family). Facts which could have been provided by MacDougall – of largely unclothed people moving, sleeping, cooking and eating in unsheltered habitats – were not considered to be of any special relevance. It is not known if these facts were asked for; if they were known to the authorities they were ignored. Even though the people at Wallatinna were only 173 km from Emu (Field, "ground zero" for Totem 1), the distinctive characteristics of their living conditions were not considered in relation to the detonation of a 10-kilotonne nuclear bomb."

In conclusion to this part of its investigations, the Royal Commission's report included these findings:

> (a) There was a failure at the Totem trials to consider adequately the distinctive lifestyle of Aborigines and, as a consequence, their special vulnerability to radioactive fallout.
>
> (b) Inadequate resources were allocated to guaranteeing the safety of Aborigines during the Totem nuclear tests.
>
> (c) The Native Patrol Officer had the impossible task of locating and warning Aborigines, some of whom lived in traditional lifestyles and were scattered over more than 100 000 square kilometres. (P.173)

Such was the conclusion drawn as to the inadequate treatment – intentional or otherwise – of Aboriginal people in the lead up to nuclear testing on their traditional lands, but what of the impact of those tests on Anangu, and by extension the Uluru family? What of this "black mist"?

Both Reggie and Alan recall the event with clarity and animation, as do others including Yami, who was 12 years old at the time of the detonation of Totem 1 at Emu Field in 1953.

Yami gave evidence at the Royal Commission, having effectively started the ball rolling some five years previously with his approach to the media in which he claimed to have lost his eyesight as a result of the nuclear testing. Medical examinations conducted on the young Yami's eyes suggested the presence of trachoma scarring, so there has always been some conjecture as to whether the "black mist" caused or added to his eventual blindness and he himself states in his autobiography that "I never did find out if one of those bombs made me blind".

Nevertheless, in giving evidence to the commission, Yami, who went on to be one of the most powerful Anangu voices in indigenous affairs, including the debate over the handback of Uluru-Kata Tjuta, said he "heard a big bang, a big noise, an explosion" and then something on the air "coming from the south, black-like smoke. I was thinking it might be a dust storm but it was quiet, just moving... through the trees and above...just rolling and moving quietly." (p. 174-175)

Others who gave evidence told of how the elders at Wallatinna were frightened by the cloud of "smoke" that rolled in following the explosion and tried to scare what they thought might have been a "mamu" (evil spirit) away from their camps with their woomeras. Yami's father Kanytji and mother Pingkayi also gave evidence, saying they heard the blast and that it was followed some time later by a smoke or mist of some sort: "...wide and fairly low on the ground... black and spreading out...with the wind pushing it...".

Some said it had a "strong smell" and almost all referred variously to people developing headaches, coughing, vomiting, diarrhoea, sore eyes, skin rashes and sores that appeared two weeks later.

Others who were at Wallatinna at the time have similar recollections:

> "That's when the sickness came, from South Australia, the atomic bomb. It flew over everywhere and our families were tired. I was a little girl and my mother and father told me I got sick too, but I was alright (because) the nurse gave me something. That big bomb down there, the wind carried over and brought it here too. And they could smell it and the kids got sick, coughing, some feeling weak, lying near the fire and

dying. Everybody, they don't know what happened. They got really sick and later on they said that's the atomic bomb in South Australia. Big mob at the cemetery, men, women and children. Not my family, other families, they died. The government came here and they say it's a sickness and they brought medicine and gave it to them. Some got better and better and some they died. After the atomic bomb we had measles."[4]

The Royal Commission's report touched on the difficulty of eliciting exact details from which to draw a conclusion as to the effects of this "black mist":

"In the Wallatinna group evidence, it was reported that people had died but because of the unique counting system of the Pitjantjatjara people and the taboos which operate about mentioning death, the numbers alleged to have died could not be ascertained. Similarly, the numbers of people actually at Wallatinna when the puyu passed could not be obtained from the people who gave evidence, but (the patrol officers') reports put the Aboriginal numbers between 30 and 40." (p.175)

The commission's investigations give yet another insight into the gulf between traditional culture and society and a prevailing observational and evidence-gathering framework that put Anangu at a significant disadvantage in the quest to be heard. The absence of written historical records to document mortality and illness or to record timelines and event dates left the commission with only anecdotal evidence. Further difficulty arose from a lack of data relating to the specific effect of exposure to radiation on the people who were at Wallatinna that fateful day, which the commission posed may well have been exacerbated by pre-existing and underlying health issues.

"There may be a probability unknown and certainly unquantified, that the Aboriginal people were in an immuno-suppressed state due to the effects of poor nutrition and the after-effects of catastrophic epidemics of introduced diseases which raged in the area for years. There may

be a probability, again unknown and unquantified, that at doses lower than otherwise recorded as producing non-stochastic injury, such injury could result from an additive or synergistic relationship between radiation exposure and other conditions such as measles or trachoma." (p.192-193)

In his autobiographical account of the event, Yami puts this conundrum simply:

"We knew what we had seen but they wanted information that we couldn't give them, and they wanted it because they knew white people would ask us questions and wouldn't believe us. We didn't know times and dates when the black mist came over. We didn't have calendars or clocks then…and we didn't have medical records because there was no clinic at Wallatinna and no white doctors treated us." (Yami, 1993, p.193-194)

As a result of its investigations, the McClelland Royal Commission found that:

1. Fallout from Totem 1 (at Emu Field) in the vicinity of Wallatinna and Welbourn Hill did exceed the limits proposed for inhabited locations. It follows that Totem 1 should not have been fired when it was.

2. The predicted and observed fallout from Totem 1 produced unacceptable levels of contamination on areas where people could be expected to be.

3. The Totem 1 test was fired under wind conditions that the study in Report A32 had shown would produce unacceptable levels of fallout. Measured fallout from Totem 1 on Inhabited regions did exceed the limits proposed in Report A32.

4. The firing criteria used for the Totem 1 test ignored some of the recommendations of Report AJ2 and did not take into account the existence of people at Wallatinna and Welbourn Hill down-wind of the test site. (P150-151)

In drawing its conclusions on the effects of nuclear testing in central Australia on Aboriginal people of the region, the commission's assessment is damning but given the absence of specific data on which to base a conclusive recommendation, the final analysis leaves many questions unanswered.

Perhaps it is fitting to leave the last word, here at least, to the late Yami Lester, brother to the Uluru family and leader to many Anangu, who returned to his Tjukurpa spirit world in July 2017:

> *"I still say our people suffered because of it (the nuclear testing), only we didn't have the times and dates and medical records. So the Royal Commission made an open finding: they said they just didn't know one way or the other if Aboriginal people at Wallatinna got sick and maybe died from the black mist. Maybe we'll always be in the dark about it. There's one thing though, white people in Australia knew a lot more about what happened on their own home ground." (Yami, P.194)*

• • • •

1. Yami: The autobiography of Yami Lester, IAD Press, 1993, P 194
2. RC Report – Annette Hamilton
3. RC Report Report of the McClelland Royal Commission into British Nuclear Testing in Australia: Australian Government Publishing Service, Commonwealth of Australia, 1985.
4. Daphne Puntjina, quoted in "Every Hill Got a Story", compiled and edited by Marg Bowman; Hardie Grant Books (Australia) 2015, p36. Note: "The Maralinga bomb testing occurred around the same time as the epidemic of measles, which resulted in many deaths of Aboriginal people in Central Australia. The timing made it difficult for people to tell what caused the sickness." – Note 7, p.261

CHAPTER 8

"We were stockmen"

Reggie and Cassidy Uluru's trademark cowboy hats shade faces lined by experience, humour and hardship and their expressive dark hands are those of men who have shaped a family, a history and the heart of their country.

Both look like they could have walked straight from the pages of Australian outback history, the living embodiment of our romantic notion of the Aboriginal stockman whose skill and dedication helped build an iconic industry. Because they were and are.

Throughout our many conversations, the Uluru brothers' memories turn fondly and often to their days in the saddle as stockmen on the vast pastoral runs of central Australia. They are proud of those days, that work and their skill. Ask any former Aboriginal stockman – Reggie, Cassidy and other Uluru family members included – and they'll tell you those were the halcyon days, among the best. Despite the rigours of that life and the impact of pastoralism on the traditional life of Anangu, it's a perhaps simpler time for which the tjilpis still yearn.

Through the prism of hindsight, it's hard to fathom how these two traditional owners and sons of Paddy Uluru could so affectionately recall their time in an industry that, as important as it has been to the national and agricultural economy, effectively destroyed much of traditional Anangu life and the landscape that sustained it for so many thousands of years.

But that contemporary judgement needs to be tempered by an understanding of Anangu resilience and an admiration for the way in which Reggie and Cassidy have accepted change and learned to adjust. While their view is far from rose-coloured, it is not their way to dwell on the past or hold grudges.

• • • •

After the overland telegraph station was established at Alice Springs in 1872, the first pastoral operations began to spring up around that fledgling service centre, gradually spreading in the ensuing years into the outer regions of Central Australia.

Some resistance was mounted by the Aboriginal inhabitants and there are historical records of conflict with white settlers, prompted by the dramatic and immediate effect of livestock on the natural resources so vital to the subsistence lifestyle of Anangu.

In 1924, the Crown Lands authorities issued leases that allowed Aboriginal access to pastoral lands for hunting and water but although well-intentioned, these pieces of paper paid lip-service only to the plight of Anangu. The impact of introduced stock had already had a significant and irreversible affect on the land. Water sources had been tapped for bores and tanks, soakages and rock-holes had been fouled by stock and camels and the introduction of cats and foxes had been devastating for populations of smaller native fauna, which were so much a part of the day-to-day sustenance of Anangu. So too, the effect of stock on the diversity and abundance of native flora had a significant impact on the plants that provided Anangu with the basis of their everyday diet.

Coupled with the effect of drought on an already fragile ecosystem, the incursion of pastoral leases had the almost immediate result of rendering a traditional existence even more fraught than it had ever been, regardless of whether Anangu were "allowed" under whitefella law to use the pastoral leases as they had since time began.

Conflict began to arise with Anangu forced through circumstance to turn to other means of surviving, specifically through spearing and eating stock that had largely replaced their traditional food sources. The Coniston massacre of 1928, in which some sixty Aboriginal men, women and children were shot and killed over a two-month period, still looms large in the minds of Anangu. This was followed in 1934 by the shooting of Paddy's brother at Uluru, and the cumulative effect was to drive many Aboriginal people from their homelands in fear.

Increasing rail access to Central Australia saw the pastoral industry's exponential expansion and between 1930 and 1950, there had been a six-fold increase in livestock numbers in the region. After 1930, white pastoral settlement began its march west into Uluru country, the first of the stations established on Yangkutatjara country being Ernabella in 1933.[1]

Within the space of just a few years, the cycle of Anangu dependence on the whitefella economy, of which they were rarely a part, had begun. Perversely, though, it was the very industry that brought about this monumental shift in Anangu history that gave the Uluru brothers, and many other Aboriginal people besides, some of the happiest times of their working lives and for the first time brought Aboriginal people into the mainstream white economy where they became an integral part of the success of the pastoral enterprises.

It would be wrong to use the rear-view mirror of contemporary context to challenge or judge when Reggie and Cassidy happily proclaim, "We were stockmen."

Reggie:

Tjilpis know a lot about being a stockman. The generation after us were painters. We were cowboys. We need to tell the young fellas and talk to them about being a stockman. What strong lives we had as stockmen! We want to get some of that skill and strength into the young fellas of today, so let's get them back on horses and learning all those things.

When we were stockmen, we used to go out bush when we were hungry. We'd grab a horse to go and hunt malu. The (white) stockmen would question us about this but they needed to understand that we were hungry. Sometimes the horse would wander off but we'd cook up our malu, eat it and then go and find the horse later.

We were droving bullocks to Oodnadatta at one time. There were no yards so we would have to watch over the bullocks at night. You'd have to be careful if you were a smoker because if the bullocks saw the light when you were lighting your smoke they'd scare and run off.

Then we went to Mimili. I remember all the old people

who were around there when I was young and they were all very good people. I remember the station people being good people too. They'd ask us, "Do you want to work?" and we'd say, "Yes!" and we'd jump in the car and they'd take us off to work. We'd hang around and watch the work and that's how we learned. I learned how to ride a horse. I was a good rider.

Sometimes we'd get a little money. A dollar, something like that. But they would pay us with supplies like flour and sugar and tea. They gave us clothes and boots and hats. They also would pay us in tobacco but I didn't smoke. The others would follow behind the car and the horses and pick up the butts the other stockmen would throw away.

When I was a stockman, we didn't use spears. We used a rifle for the bullocks. We made hobbles for the horses, we didn't make spears. I made ropes too. I was good at making ropes.

I went on a big trip droving cattle to Queensland. We went from Henbury Station just south of Alice Springs and we took the cattle down to Todd Morden Station, just this side of Coober Pedy. That was a long trip. And all the while we had to watch the cattle because there were no yards to keep them in as we travelled. You had to watch them at night. And you'd have to be very careful with things like making a light at night, like with a match for a smoke, because it would frighten the cattle and that's very dangerous because they would stampede.

When we were droving, we would have to find water for the bullocks. We had to show the whitefellas where the water was. And even if that water was dirty, we would still fill our canteens. Sometimes we walked. Sometimes we were on horses.

Sometimes there would be fights between the stockmen and they'd end up in fisticuffs. That's when we'd decide, hey, we're going. We're leaving. And we'd pack up and go. Sometimes we'd try to take the horses but they'd always say, "Hey – you can't take those horses. You go but you leave the horses behind." And we'd say, "No, it'll be right. We'll bring them back. I'd get the horse back to the station. So sometimes I'd get back to the station and they'd say, "Hey, where's everyone else?" and I'd say, "Oh, I left them back there because they were fighting. There was an argument and I got frightened so I left." But I would always take the horse back.

Cassidy:

I was a good stockman. I enjoyed being a stockman. I had a full belly and it was good work. And I had a big hat, I remember that (laughs). When I was a young fella, a wati, I liked riding horses. You had to be strong to roll the bullocks and brand them. I was strong then – but not now.

I went to work on the station at Mimili (Everard Park) as a young fella after my mum and dad grew me up. I was strong then but not so strong now. I worked on Everard Park and Granite Downs and De Rose Hill Station, mustering bullock. Mimili was the first community that we started fighting for, to take it back over from the cattle station. That's when Indulkana became a community, because it was also a cattle station. I worked up into Queensland as well, on stations as a stockman working with bullocks.

Ration days were good. We would get sugar, flour, tea, milk – it was really good. We ate dingo too. It was strong meat, good meat. We would also eat kangaroo and bush goanna, but I don't eat ngintaka because it's my dreaming. We weren't allowed to eat the bullocks either.

The station owners would give us all our clothes – belt, hat, trousers, boots – and tobacco and food. They looked after the old people, too. When we picked up our rations we would walk from the homestead to our camp, about three kilometres. No motor car.

The manager of Everard Park Station was my boss. He looked after all the cattle and the stock. He was the boss man.

He had a lot of land to look after. He was a good man.

I used to go to the races, but I didn't ride the horses in the races. I went to the Mount Isa rodeo, too. I didn't ride in the rodeo – I'm smart! I just watch them.

For all his fond memories, Reggie recalls that, at times, being an Aboriginal stockman could be a precarious existence. It's a sentiment recollected elsewhere by others who lived through those tough and sometimes perilous times when the Central Australian cattle industry was still a wild and unpredictable frontier.

All I know is that we learned, "Yes boss, no boss". Whenever we did a job, don't be told twice. When they tell you once, you do it. If there is some job you don't need to be told, you do it anyway, that sort of thing – and you're a good man. And if you talk back you're not worth feeding cocky shit, not worth feeding on greenhide. You're a good man if you don't talk back. Yes boss, no boss.[2]

Reggie:

We were frightened of the whitefella stockmen's whips. We thought they might whip us. They did that to teach us that it was not okay to steal, but we didn't know what stealing was. We were still learning that you couldn't take other people's things. So they would crack the whip to teach us not to take other people's things because that is stealing. We worked well. We didn't steal anything.

In those early days there were quite a few (whitefella) stockmen who were really cruel to Anangu. Very aggressive and cranky.

Sometimes we'd be hunted off by stockmen on a horse or say the stockmen were out riding on horses and they would come across a group of Anangu who were just walking out on country, and the stockmen would say, "Hey, who are you? Where are you from?" but those poor blokes (Anangu) didn't understand what the whitefellas were saying. Maybe they had (unintentionally) done something that had scared or scattered the bullocks or maybe the stockmen thought they might do something, and the stockmen would chase them away with whips. They would chase them on horseback, using their whips. And the Anangu didn't know what was wrong or what was happening, so they were frightened and that made them not so friendly.

That worked both ways. Sometimes the Anangu were cranky too. When there were good people (both whitefella and Anangu) involved then things were usually okay. But sometimes arguments started (among Anangu). Maybe for instance like over rations. If the whitefellas had the food and gave it to the Anangu who had been working, gave it to the workers, then sometimes other Anangu (not the workers) weren't happy with that. They didn't understand about the connection between work and food or the idea of payment of food in return for working. They weren't thinking that way so they expected to have a share because in Anangu culture everything is shared.

They didn't understand how things worked in the whitefella way so they got cranky and fights started.

Throughout the '50s and '60s, while Reggie and Cassidy were working on cattle stations as stockmen, actual monetary pay for Aboriginal employees was still a way off. It was not until 1968 that the Conciliation and Arbitration Commission ruled for equal wages in the cattle industry, but the decision is often considered a hollow victory. Station owners had been for decades "paying" their Aboriginal employees with rations and clothing, often also supporting whole extended families, and pastoralists warned the commission that if they were forced to pay Aboriginal workers, they would instead employ white workers.[3]

This is precisely what happened, and many Aboriginal stockmen were no longer employed on the stations. In many cases, families and entire communities were evicted from the stations where they had lived and worked for years and where, it must be said, Anangu had traditionally lived for millennia. Often, they drifted to the fringes of the towns where they were given what they still refer to as "sit down money", or welfare. In many regards, this represented not only a great loss of self-esteem but an equally destructive disconnection, for men in particular, from their obligations to Tjukurpa and country.

> The idea of working is that through your own labour, through your own efforts, you are feeding yourself. You are looking after your family not waiting for someone else to look after you. Like in the old days, no one would do it for you. You had to do the work yourself. Should be same now.[4]

While the granting of equal pay was indeed a triumph for the civil rights movement which gained so much important ground during the late '60s and early '70s[*], the long-term consequences were, as they so often are, not always as positive as anticipated.

Perhaps this helps in a roundabout way to explain why Reggie and Cassidy lament so deeply the loss of those days when Anangu could proudly proclaim, "I am a stockman".

• • • •

[*] *The 1966 Wave Hill "walk off" as it has become known was a significant milestone in Australian indigenous rights. It began as a protest by Aboriginal workers, led by head stockman Vincent Lingiari, on the giant Wave Hill Station, at the time one of the largest pastoral leases in the Northern Territory. It began as a protest against working conditions and the inequity of wages, but evolved into a landmark land rights claim for the Gurindji people.*

1. Uluru: An Aboriginal history of Ayers Rock – Robert Layton, Australian Institute of Aboriginal Studies, 1986 – p. 61-62
2. Collaborating for Indigenous Rights – National Museum of Australia, 2007-2014
3. Every hill got a story – Central Land Council, 2015 - p. 77
4. Alan Wilson, interview at Mutitjulu, March 2017

CHAPTER 9

"Uwa, they were dangerous times"

It had already been a long warm day, but Jimmy* didn't care. He was happy to trot along behind the boss' horse, his bare calloused feet keeping pace with the big chestnut mare's languid stride.

The boss had given him boots to wear, but the hard leather hurt his feet and besides, he was well used to walking this country with nothing between the earth of his homeland and his soles. The trousers, on the other hand, were proper handy with pockets for putting things in, and he wore them happily against his pitch-black skin.

Jimmy and his family had walked in off country to camp on the station when the big, long dry spell began to dry up the waterholes and when the station's fences made hunting for tucker a bit tricky. The malu and emu and all the other animals also seemed to have walked off country, and the whitefellas got proper cranky when blackfellas speared and ate the cattle.

But at the station, the boss gave them rations of flour and tea and sugar and salt meat that helped keep their bellies full. It was good tucker. Easy tucker. Jimmy and the other men would hunt when they could. Ngintaka (lizard) was good eating and seemed not to take much notice of the whitefella's changes to the land, so they were still pretty easy to find. And fun to chase.

Today, the boss and one of his stockmen were out checking the waterholes and keeping an eye on the thirsty cattle gathered around the shrinking soaks. Jimmy went along to help. The boss needed his knowledge of the landscape and where to find kapi (water) and Jimmy was as pleased as Punch that he could share what he knew about his country.

He didn't understand English but he was learning. He'd already mastered the most important words: "Yes, boss. No, boss."

A shout brought Jimmy's attention back to the moment. He looked up to see the stockman spurring his horse into a gallop across the red earth in pursuit of a calf. Jimmy watched in fascination as the stockman wielded his greenhide rope in a high loop and hurled it towards the fleeing young beast, catching the startled calf expertly in a noose at the base of its budding horns. The horse skidded to a stop on its haunches, holding the rope taught as the stockman quickly tied it to the saddle and leapt from his mount. Within seconds, the grinning stockman had bound the calf's legs, rendering it still and panting in the red dust.

"Bloody perfect," said the boss, swinging down from atop his own horse. "Now, let's get those balls off. Dunno how we missed it at the last marking."**

The boss knelt beside the calf and with one hand lifted its back leg to reveal a burgeoning set of testicles. With the other hand, he stretched around to his hip in an automatic reach for the place where his razor-sharp pocket knife usually sat ready for just such occasions.

It wasn't there. Surprised, the boss loosened his grip on the calf's leg and stood, glancing around and slapping his pockets in vain for the knife.

"Where's m'fucken' knife?" he asked of no-one in particular. He looked at his stockman. "Where's my fucken' knife?"

"Dunno, boss. Maybe you dropped it. Here, use mine," said the wiry offsider, reaching into the leather pouch at his belt and holding out his own pocketknife.

The boss, clearly cranky, snatched the knife and opened it, flicking his thumb across the blade.

"You couldn't cut butter with this fucken' knife," he growled. "I'm not gonna mark a calf with that – I need my fucken' knife."

The stockman, sensing the boss' growing temper, said nothing.

"Jimmy!" roared the boss.

"Yes, boss," said Jimmy with a grin. He didn't know what a "fucken' knife" was but he figured he was about to find out.

"You bin got boss fucken' knife?"

"No, boss."

The boss sighed in frustration and swept an irritated gaze from left to right across the view from the four-mile waterhole, then back towards the direction of the homestead.

"Jimmy, you go get boss fucken' knife. Go find my wife. Find missus. You tell her, boss bin need pocket-knife. You bin get 'im? Plenty hurry."

"Yes, boss," said Jimmy, puffing out his chest with pride. The boss was giving him a job. Jimmy wasn't sure exactly what that job was, but he reckoned he could work it out as he went along. "Yes, boss."

The stockman spat a long stream of saliva into the dust beside him. "Boss, he doesn't have a clue what you're talking about. I'll go get it."

"No, you stay here. He'll be right. It's only four miles and these blackfellas are fast. We'll check the other stock while he's gone."

The boss turned to Jimmy. "You bin understand, Jimmy? I bin need pocketknife," he said, gesturing and gesticulating in an effort to reinforce his pidgin instructions. "You run plenty fast, no stop, find my wife, find missus, tell 'im boss need knife."

Jimmy nodded. "Yes, boss. Fucken' knife."

The stockman and the boss hooted with laughter and even though he didn't understand what was so funny, Jimmy was well pleased at being tasked with such an important job, and he laughed too.

"That's right Jimmy, fucken' knife," said the boss, still laughing. "Find wife. Tell missus, need pocketknife. Now go. Run plenty fast. Only little bit long way, you come back plenty fast, yes?"

"Yes, boss."

"You no stop, eh?"

"No, boss."

Jimmy's feet barely touched the ground as he set off at a run back towards the homestead. This was a big job, an important job for the boss. Maybe if he did this job proper way, the boss might let him learn to ride a horse.

Then he could climb up into the saddle like a proper blackfella stockman, with a proper hat. He would ride high and swing that rope

Paddy Uluru,
c. 1978.
*Source: Ara Irititja,
Nyangatjatjara
College collection*

Paddy Uluru with dingo scalps, 1964. Source: Ara Irititja, Bushridge and Culhane collection

Paddy Uluru brought his family, including sons Reggie and Cassidy, back to Uluru in the late 1950s after being in Mimili for two decades since the shooting of his brother at Uluru in 1934. This photo is much treasured by the family – it shows Cassidy (aged around seven or eight) to the left of his father, and Reggie (a teenager at the time) to the right. *Photo: supplied by the family, but believed to have been taken from an image that appeared in Bill Harney's 1959 book, Tales from the Aborigines, p.177)*

Cassidy Uluru looks fondly at the photo of his father Paddy bringing his family back to Uluru from exile at Mimili. It was the first time Cassidy and Reggie had seen the rock. *Photo: Jen Cowley, 2016*

Cassidy Uluru with the Mutitjulu Community bus, c.1980.
Source: Ara Irititja, John Hill and Jo Wynter collection

Cassidy Uluru sits atop Willy Kumantjara's winning horse, Black Betty, at the Marla races in 1990. Willy was the winning jockey.
Source: Ara Irititja, Margaret Dinham collection

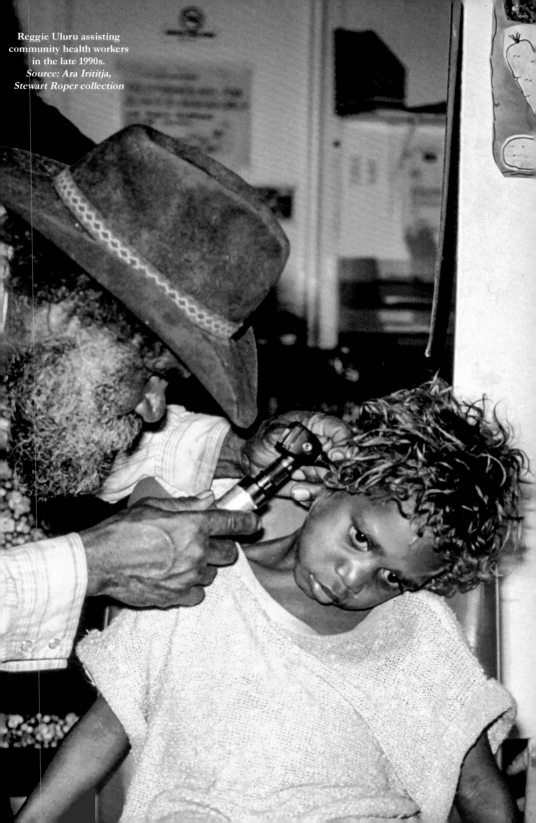

Reggie Uluru assisting
community health workers
in the late 1990s.
*Source: Ara Irititja,
Stewart Roper collection*

LtoR: Nipper Winmati, Yami Lester (chair of Pitjantjatjara Council), Reggie Uluru, Clyde Holding (Minister for Aboriginal Affairs) and Ngalitjanu Dickie Minyintiri at a meeting of the Pitjantjatjara Council at Mutitjulu, c. 1983-5. *Source: Ara Irititja, Pitjantjatjara Council collection*

Reggie Uluru (second from left) and Yami Lester (centre) at the ceremony for the handback of the Uluru-Kata Tjuta National Park to the Anangu, October 26, 1985. *Source: Ara Irititja, Jim and Shirley Downing collection*

Andrew Uluru and Tiku Captain (wife of Cassidy Uluru) with the NT Tourism Brolga Encouragement Award won by Anangu Tours in the late 1990s. *Photo: Ara Irititja, Nyangatjatjara College collection*

Cassidy Uluru and his wife Tiku Captain as guides with Anangu Tours at Uluru, in the late 1990s. *Photo: supplied by family*

Paddy Uluru's grave in the shadow of the great rock,
at Mutitjulu cemetery. *Photo: Jen Cowley*

Cassidy Uluru, Alan Wilson and Reggie Uluru at Paddy's Camp, near Mutitjulu, 2017. *Photo: Jen Cowley*

Cassidy Uluru, Sammy Wilson (Tjama Uluru), Tjiangu (TJ) Thomas and Reggie Uluru, at the launch of community project photo book, Anangu Wai, at Yulara in 2016. *Photo: Steve Cowley*

Cassidy and Reggie Uluru at Paddy's Camp near Mutitjulu, 2017. *Photo: Jen Cowley*

Project interpreter Kathryn ("kt") Tozer with partner Sammy Wilson (Tjama Uluru), examining maps to help plot the course of Paddy Uluru's journey back to Uluru from Mimili in the late 1950s.
Photo: Taken at Mutitjulu in 2017, Jen Cowley

Carnett Brumby-Churchill with the front page of the Koori Mail showing his grandfather Sammy
Wilson's (Tjama Uluru's) announcement of the impending closure of the Uluru climb, 2017.
Photo: Jonathon Hill

Sammy Wilson (Tjama Uluru) with Kathryn ("kt") Tozer at Patji, 2018. *Photo: Jen Cowley*

Uluru WH

12KM

1KM PATJI RH

TJAPIYA

33KM

UNTIAI S

28KM

ALPARA B
12KM

WILU WH.

NT
SA

WIPITA S

1KM

12KM

MULGA PK HS

1KM

(ROCKET BORE)
WANA HILLA

97KM

"WH NEAR BIG ROCK"
PROBABLY NGARUTJARA

ERNABELLA - "CANNED FOR A WHILE"

35KM

YUNYARINYI
(KENMORE PK HS)

25KM

WINPIRA B

44 KM

ATUTJA RH

Mimili 12 KM

B = BORE
RH = ROCK HOLE
S = SOAK.
WH = WATER HOLE
HS = HOMESTEAD
Not to scale - Distances aprox (Total 358 KM).

just like he'd seen the other stockmen do. He would chase and rope the bullocks. He would go droving. He would be a proper stockman and he would be important and his family would be happy and he could teach his own sons one day and...

And what was it the boss had told him? Fucken' knife? Wiya... find wife? Get fucken' knife? Pocket knife. Uwa, that was it.

As he ran, Jimmy chanted over and over to himself, "Fucken' knife. Tell missus pocketknife... pocketknife...fucken knife...find wife...pocketknife..."

He was determined he would do this job proper way and the boss would be pleased.

On and on he ran across the red dunes and spinifex, mumbling the words over and over as he went until, from the side of his vision, the swift movement of a ngintaka caught his eye. Jimmy's stride didn't falter. He darted off in pursuit of the lizard, his mission momentarily forgotten by the siren call of good tucker. But the fleet footed reptile was too fast. Jimmy launched himself at full stretch towards the ngintaka's whipping tail as it disappeared down a hole, his grasp missing by mere inches.

Jimmy stood, dusting himself off and cursing for the lack of a spear. Suddenly, he remembered why he didn't have his spear with him and grimaced at his foolish distraction. He had wasted precious minutes and would have to run even faster now to reach the homestead and... what was it he was supposed to say to the missus? Something like "find my wife"? "Fucken wife"? Wiya, "pocket knife"? Wiya, "fucken' knife". Uwa, that was it. Wife. Fucken' knife.

He loped on through the bush, picking up speed and panting in the late afternoon heat until the fence of the homestead paddock finally came into view. He reached the gate and leant against its post to try to collect his thoughts and recall the boss' instructions. Taking deep gulps of air, Jimmy wished he could stop for a drink of water, but that would have to wait. This was an important job. He would not let the boss down. He would do this job proper way and please the boss.

As he crossed the thirsty dust of the house yard, the boss' wife appeared at the top of the verandah steps, wiping her hands on the floral fabric of her apron.

"What is it, Jimmy?"

Still panting, Jimmy stood to his full height and stammered.

"Missus…boss says…"

"Yes, Jimmy. What is it? What's wrong?" said the boss' wife with growing alarm.

Jimmy stared blankly at the stout, stern-faced missus, desperately searching his mind for the right English words, trying to recall exactly what the boss had told him.

"Boss says… boss says…"

Now clearly irritated, the missus put her hands on her hips and demanded.

"Jimmy, you tell me now. WHAT does the boss say?"

Suddenly, Jimmy grinned. He had it. He remembered what the boss had told him to say.

"Missus, boss says… fuck my wife."

• • • •

Reggie punctuates the telling of this story with a characteristic chuckle that is utterly infectious and, as awful as it is, I can't help laughing along at the awkwardness of the tale's punchline.

Until his next words stop my mirth dead in my throat.

"They shot him, that bloke."

Suddenly, the story is no longer funny.

> That's a true story, that one. That man, they shot him. They killed him, that Anangu man. Because he had no English, I think. He did the wrong thing for the woman, so that's why he got squared back. Young wati did the wrong thing but only because of no English. And maybe as he was walking he got distracted by a ngintaka or something and that's how he forgot the word "pocketknife". So instead of asking for the pocketknife, he asked for something very different.

Throughout the gathering of information and recollections for the retelling of the Uluru family story, it has been patently and at times painfully apparent just how quickly a bridge of cultural trust can be burned by an accidental misunderstanding of linguistic nuance. As awkward as that can be, for those on both sides of the language divide, it is highly unlikely that even the direst of slips would these days result in mortal danger. The same cannot be said of the early days of contact and colonisation and well into the mid-twentieth century, where the gap between traditional language and English could be a perilous abyss for both black and white.

Many a tale is told of how these misunderstandings, particularly in a swiftly changing social and cultural climate of suspicion and fear, could have tragic consequences. Some are more stomach churning than others:

Reggie:

They were dangerous times when we were kids.

This story is something that happened when Anangu did the wrong thing. The whitefella would say to the wati (young man), you dig this hole here. And the wati would dig the hole and then they would make him jump down into the hole. And the whitefella would fill that hole with kerosene and then set it alight with fire.

There are lots of stories of this happening.

Maybe this is what happened when someone (Anangu) did the wrong thing maybe because they didn't understand the English. They didn't understand the words and that's why they did the wrong thing or something was wrong way.

I remember seeing this when I was a tjitji – a wati digging a hole and this is why, because he'd done the wrong thing. We didn't know. We didn't say anything because we were just kids. Anangu got into trouble in those days because of no English. Whitefellas and Anangu couldn't understand each other sometimes.

Uwa, they were dangerous times.

The perilous confusion over language worked both ways. Another incident, recounted by Uluru family members, involved the simple misunderstanding of a single word, "kanpi", which is the word for emu fat and also the name for a sacred place of significant men's business for those of the emu Tjukurpa. A wati (young man) kept hearing a whitefella say what he thought was the word, "kanpi", when in fact the man was saying "can't be". Said quickly, "can't be" sounded to the wati like the man was saying "kanpi", and therefore deeply disrespecting a sacred facet of men's business.

To Anangu, this is a crime punishable by death. Tjukurpa demanded the wati carry out his responsibilities under traditional law to punish such sacrilege. The wati speared and killed the whitefella, as necessary under Tjukurpa, but ran away in fear of reprisal. Traditional law deemed the killing just. Piranpa law, of course, saw it as murder.

Alan Wilson recalls a similar story, whereby his grandfather found himself branded a murderer for fatally spearing a whitefella he found bathing in the waterhole of a place that was deeply sacred under men's business. The white man was blatantly breaking traditional law, a crime so serious as to be deemed punishable by death. The Anangu man, true to his Tjukurpa, had no choice but to abide by his law, lest he himself be accused of breaking it.

As the white man submerged himself in the sacred water to complete his ablutions, Alan's grandfather crept up alongside the waterhole. When the man emerged after rinsing his body, the Anangu man used his spear to kill him.

"That was right for him to do. In fact, Tjukurpa says he had no choice but to do that," Alan explained. "But under Piranpa law, my grandfather was a murderer."

These are by no means isolated accounts of how the clash of language and culture brought Anangu law into direct conflict with the prevailing white laws of the day. It's a divide that remains almost as wide today as it did then and although the consequences are perhaps less immediately fatal, they can be no less catastrophic for the long-term structure of Anangu society.

The overrepresentation of Aboriginal people, young men in

particular, in Australia's corrective services system is a national tragedy, and much debate has been waged as to the root cause of this glaring imbalance.

But as it relates to the Uluru family's story, much of the disparity can be traced back to the destructive cultural abyss between traditional and contemporary law into which so many Anangu fall.

Sammy:

For instance, women never used to use certain words that only belonged to men. That was traditional law. Now they swear using those words. Some Anangu are in jail because their women used those words.

It's still happening, that divide between traditional law and white law because, for instance, to use certain words to swear at a man is a really, really high degree offence that in the past you'd be speared for. But now women are using those words and provoking an assault. The men try to control their response because they know assault is an offence under white law, but under traditional law, the offence is the use of those words and is therefore punishable. But the women keep provoking them with these words so the men end up assaulting them. Then the woman goes to the police and the men end up in jail for assault. So the whitefella law is carrying out justice, but there's no sense of justice in terms of the traditional law.

Sammy stresses that he is by no means justifying violence against women, Anangu or otherwise. He is not excusing, he is explaining. He also explains that there are far less serious offences under whitefella law that see so many Anangu fall foul of it.

The gaols 'round these parts of Australia are full of Anangu who are behind bars for what most of us would see as relatively minor traffic infringements, but they are "crimes" repeated often by Anangu who simply don't see driving unregistered cars around country without a license as an offence.

The imposition of laws around road use, registration and licenses bear little relevance for people whose connection to traditional culture and Tjukurpa is still so strong. The whitefella laws have significantly hampered people's ability to stay connected to country.

Access to licenses*** and registration for their cars is limited, but the Anangu imperative to travel their country and to other country to connect with family is far stronger than their consciousness of whitefella law. It is simply inconceivable that Anangu would neglect their obligation under Tjukurpa to visit family or mob simply because they don't have a piece of paper or there's a broken window in the car.

To law-abiding whitefellas, this might seem like a cavalier disregard for the laws of the land. And thereby hangs the problem. To Anangu, cultural laws trump piranpa rules.

Similarly, the absence under Tjukurpa of any sense of maintaining or owning property has brought Anangu asunder when it comes to the letter of piranpa law. For thousands of years, there had been no sense under traditional culture of owning let alone maintaining property, and the notion of caring for material things is still somewhat foreign. Property, therefore, is fair game when there is no overarching idea of ownership and the whitefella law takes a dim view – as it did back in the early days of pastoralism – of what it would call "stealing". Anangu call it sharing.

The obligation of traditional law is still very much a part of Anangu society, however discussion of the imposition of penalties and the nuances of those laws remains the preserve of those charged with their protection. Suffice to say that two centuries have not been anywhere near long enough for the white man's law to snuff out tens of thousands of years of Tjukurpa's command. That the gulf between the two laws and languages continues to create conflict both emotional and social is another valid reason for the veil of secrecy that surrounds the meting out of traditional law.

The language barrier has also had demonstrably disastrous consequences for white society, such as in the case of the tragic disappearance at Uluru of baby Azaria Chamberlain. The two-month-old girl vanished from her parents' tent at the base of the rock in 1980, taken it was claimed at the time, by a dingo. The tragedy sparked an extraordinary case that continues to capture the world's attention more than three decades later.

The murder and accessory to murder charges laid against the child's parents were quashed in 1988 with the Supreme Court of Darwin proclaiming them innocent, but leaving an open finding as to the cause of death. After the fourth inquest in 2012 – a staggering thirty-two years after Azaria disappeared (her remains have never been found) – the Northern Territory Coroner's office declared what eyewitnesses and those Anangu who had been part of the initial search had known all along: that a dingo had taken the baby.

Much of the thirty-year heartache, angst and legal wrangling over the case may well have been avoided had the accounts and testimony of Anangu witnesses been taken seriously, or indeed considered at all, at the time.

Some of the elders living now at Mutitjulu remember and were involved in the initial search for the missing infant. One, who was part of the search party, tells of her fury at the judge in Darwin who was saying "ridiculous things" about the habits of dingoes. She says she just laughed at him and he refused to listen to her when she challenged his statements.

One of the Mutitjulu-based Anangu trackers engaged to try to find Azaria in those first few hours and days had his testimony all but ignored by the court, despite his insight and experience being, literally, second to none when it came to the landscape around the rock and the behaviour of dingoes.

The challenge arose as a result of a language barrier that meant the trackers explanation was misinterpreted as mystical mumbo jumbo by a judge who was interested only in "the facts". The tracker and other witnesses had tried to explain the behaviour of dingoes using the creation story of the Devil Dog coming to Uluru from Docker River, the intent being to illustrate that dingoes could indeed be vicious creatures.

Because of the way Anangu think about the world in terms of

connection with Tjukurpa, it was clear that there was some kind of devilishness in this dog; that the dog had an evil spirit that meant it could harm a baby. In whitefella interpretation, they were telling the court that, yes, it is entirely conceivable that a dingo would, could and most likely did take that child and harm or kill it.

The judge could not take this leap, insisting instead that the Anangu witnesses draw a distinct line in what he saw as a clear case of fact versus fiction. He was asking, through an interpreter, for the Anangu to draw a distinction between the physical, "real life" dingo and the "mythological" Tjukurpa ancestral creation story dog. The tracker and his fellow witnesses kept saying "It's the same thing – they are one."

Their attempts at explanation fell on culturally deaf ears. The judge determined that the witnesses could not separate fact from fantasy and so discredited the testimony. The whitefella court just couldn't reconcile the Anangu explanation and discounted what, with the benefit of hindsight, was vital evidence.

The travesty of this outcome is clear to anyone who has ever spent time with Anangu and has seen just how much can be determined from a set of tracks such as were followed after the child was snatched by the dingo; how much real evidence they would have been able to piece together from following those prints.

It would be cold comfort to the Chamberlain family but it would be nice to think that now, in more enlightened times, the testimony of the Anangu who know this country so intimately might be taken not only seriously, but as a first resort.

• • • •

That language is the core of culture is indisputable and it has been an edifying experience to be at the mercy of translation for the duration of this lengthy storytelling process. As an exclusively English-speaking Australian, it is humbling and deeply sobering indeed to be largely without the benefit of verbal communication when spending time with the Anangu…in the heart of my own nation. But it has been equally fascinating to learn of the depth of language's influence on an evolving society and its culture.

These insights have been made possible with the help of our interpreter, who has shared a number of thoughts over the course of our time together.****

> I've made an interesting observation about language and sense of self and culture. When I first came here, all the young ones would say, "I name is…" Now I've noticed they're saying "My name is…".
>
> There's a shift going on. I learned when I first came here that it's not "my hand", it's "I hand". In other words, we're all part of the same thing: I'm not separate from my hand – we are one and the same.
>
> It's the same concept as with country. When people talk about country, they use the word for a person. They say, "Who is your country?" not "What is your country?" If that language changes to the English way, it's a move away from your country being your spirit, being you. It creates a disconnect. It's using the same kind of word as you'd use for "table" for instance – for an inanimate object. It turns country into a "thing" rather than part of you.
>
> Whitefellas say "What is your name?" or "What is that called?" – but when you talk in Pitjantjatjara or Ngaanyatjarra about people, you use different words than you'd do for inanimate object.

There is something deeply moving about the idea of the country, the landscape, as a living thing – an entity. Conversely, it is intensely unsettling to realise how quickly and profoundly a change in language can impact that visceral connection to country. This is particularly so for the younger generations.

Even the subtlest of shifts towards English and its vernacular is potentially creating a disconnection between Anangu and their country. It is moving towards a different mindset and away from the traditional sense of country as part of person or of people and country being one and the same. That subtle change has happened only in the past few years – a blindingly fast shift for a 60,000-year-old language and culture.

As a journalist, it's second nature to ask direct questions to elicit recollections and information and in trying to piece together a personal story; asking questions about feelings is the default approach. However, not only is direct questioning not part of the way in which Anangu gather information – learning comes from immersion and listening rather than questioning – it is also important to note, again, that the word "feelings" is very difficult to translate accurately.

Neither is hindsight part of the Anangu way, so asking for reflections is difficult and it is a tricky exercise to elicit recollections of what Anangu were thinking at any particular time.

White people, particularly white storytellers, tend to analyse everything; to look for the "whys" and to seek answers to questions. Anangu preoccupations and world views are markedly different and this is reflected often in the straddling of the linguistic divide.

> For instance, it's not "just travelling around" – it's not "just". There's no Anangu word for "just" in the "simply" sense. When Anangu say they were travelling around, whitefellas tend to say, "Oh, okay, you were just moving around from place to place". But to Anangu, there was and is always a purpose to moving around. Like Sammy says, if something was happening over here, they would go there and deal with that. Then something would happen over there and they would need to be there to be part of that or do that thing.
>
> It's still hard for whitefellas to conceive of this. Remember that whitefellas need a lot of language (English) to communicate because they don't always know each other. Their way to know about each other and the world around them and how to relate to it is to ask questions.
>
> It's different for Anangu. If you're moving all through here (indicates back and forth across the map) and hearing all

the stories and being part of that whole social network, then you meet someone and you know them. You might only have met them once, but you know all about them and they know all about you. There's no need for all that small talk whitefellas need – there's no "How are you? What are you doing? Where are you from? What do you do for a crust?" It's all just there – it's all just absorbed.

This was perfectly illustrated by listening to the way Anangu answer their phones. Instead of the whitefella way of saying, "Who's calling?", Anangu will more commonly say, "Where are you calling from?" It goes to that sense of belonging to country, and of country providing identification. Again, our interpreter explains:

> Whitefellas tend to identify themselves when they ring someone. "Hi, it's so and so..." I used to do that when I first came here, but now I find myself saying "Ngayuluna Mutitjululanguru" ("It's me from Mutitjulu..."), so I've become used to that way also. That goes back to having your sense of identity drawn from country. The language reflects so much of the social structure.

And that's the crux of so much of the challenge facing those who, like the Uluru family, are charged with the sacred duty of preserving culture. For elders like Sammy, a realist who is straddling that cultural divide as a matter of necessity, the maintenance of language is everything.

There are moves afoot, and gaining momentum, to reintroduce traditional languages into schools and to preserve these ancient central and western-desert tongues before they are all but lost, as has happened elsewhere with Australia's indigenous languages. But elders like Reggie justifiably fear the damage may already have been done.

"I never went to school. I didn't learn too much English. But some people who learned that bible, I've already heard some of them denounce Tjukurpa."

While his grasp of English is far greater than his uncle's, Sammy is similarly heart-sick at the thought of language being lost:

"No stories, no culture. No language, no culture. If we don't have language, what have we got to bargain with?" he says. "Schools should be teaching tjitji the language because while ever we have language, our culture will survive."

Such is the power of language to hurt or to heal.

• • • •

This is the creative re-telling of a story recalled by Reggie. The actual name of the Anangu man involved is not known.

** *"Marking" refers to the process of castrating young male calves.*

*** *In 2014, a group of Anangu from Docker River, for whom English is a third or fourth or even fifth language, arrived in Yulara to sit for their driving licenses, prompted by a spate of arrests for unlicensed driving. They were informed they could sit the test in English and in every language from Arabic to Chinese but not in the native tongues of their homelands or the land on which Yulara sits. They were told an interpreter would have to be flown in from Darwin at great expense. After much wrangling on the part of the whitefella who had arranged for the trip in from Docker River to enable the Anangu to get their licenses, a local interpreter was located to enable the tests to be completed in the languages of the APY/NPY lands. They all gained their driving licenses.*

**** *Apart from enabling conversations through her expert interpretations, Kathy "kt" Tozer (who prefers her initials not be capitalised), offered invaluable insights and cultural observations to enrich understanding of the Uluru family's story. kt is partner to Sammy Wilson and is therefore a part of the family, but she is acutely conscious of not confusing the two roles and of remaining true to the objectivity of the interpreting process. When offering insights, kt was always careful to advise that she was speaking as an observer rather than interpreter, sometimes even physically switching chairs so as to define the two distinctly different roles.*

CHAPTER 10

"The gift of knowledge"

He loved to hunt, this young fella. It was his favourite way to spend his days, practicing all the things his grandfathers and uncles were teaching him and showing him; walking the country of his family; placing his feet in their footsteps, stepping towards the time when he too would become a man. One day.

This was his country. He belonged to this land, this place where one day he too would take the baton of his Tjukurpa and learn the secrets that would be his to know and his to pass on when he had sons of his own. One day.

Not this day, though. This day he would go hunting. This day, he would practice being a man. And this day he and his friend had a truck! A rare treat. This day they would be able to hunt many malu and this night he would proudly help feed his family – just like a man would – with a feast of malu (kangaroo). This day would bring him closer to being a man. This day.

The sun had woken and spread its warmth across the earth as the young friends bounced happily out of camp in the borrowed truck, peering all the while through the dusty windscreen as the red tracks of the desert took them further and further across country.

Desert oaks and mulga, sand-dunes and tjanpi, ridges and rocks and dry creek beds – the land rolled past under an endless canopy of blue summer sky, telling an ancient story as it went.

The sun was beginning its steady slide towards day's end when, in the distance, the youngsters saw the tell-tale movement of malu and, whooping with youthful glee for the coming chase, sent the old truck's weary tyres bouncing across the plain in pursuit.

The chase was short lived. With a lurch and a cough, the truck chugged to a stop and the lads' wide eyes met.

As the tails of the startled malu whipped a retreat through the desert, the young hunters raised the truck's bonnet and stared at the dust covered engine as if some miracle might reveal itself to set them again on their way.

Nothing.

"Did you put fuel in it?"

"Wiya. Did you?"

"Wiya."

The young fella slammed the hood down and clambered up over the truck to stand on its roof, feeling the heat of the sun-warmed steel beneath his bare feet.

He looked out across the desert, turning slowly in a full circle in search of some landmark with which to gauge their situation.

The shadows were creeping across the country, reaching out to take the last of the day. It would be foolish to try to find their way back in the dark. They would stay where they were for this night.

Perhaps they could make a campfire but, wiya, what would be the point? They had nothing to cook. No malu. No perentie. He cursed his rashness. He still had much to learn.

He fell asleep looking up at the night sky and wondered, as his stomach rumbled, if the eyes of those Anangu ancestors peering back at him were twinkling with laughter at his folly.

The pair set off as the new day cracked open, leaving the traitorous truck and its empty fuel tank behind them in what would likely be its rusty desert grave. They would walk to a place not far away where they knew they would find kapi (water) and from there, they should be able to draw on what they had already learned of country to find their way home.

Their thirst quenched for a time, the two walked on, their bare-footed steps growing slower and more measured as the sun rose up and across the cloudless sky.

"We can't be too far away," the lad told himself, feeling the grumbles from his empty belly grow louder with each step.

They walked on and on. Their thirst and hunger grew. So did the first tickles of fear.

Just as he was beginning to think his hunger would beat him home, the young fella saw a bush, shining like a beacon in the red sand. Bush tomatoes! He fell to his knees and plucked at the silvery leaves, filling his mouth and the pockets of his shorts with the small round beads of salvation.

"Here," he said to his companion, reaching out a fistful of the tucker.

"Bit green," his mate replied, popping a couple of the little native fruits into his mouth but waving away the offer of more.

Yes, they could be a bit riper, thought the young fella, but he was hungry. So hungry.

He chewed as they walked, stopping to fill his pockets each time he saw the pale green of the bush tomato plant.

Soon the sun was high in the sky and relentless in its heat. Their feet had already carried them many miles that day and still they seemed no closer to home.

The young fella's stomach again began to rumble but this time its protest was different and growing more urgent with each step. He tried to swallow but his mouth was a sandy void and he could raise no spit.

The landscape began to swoon before his eyes and his young body swayed in time with the shimmering heat.

"Hey! Hey!" he heard the voice of his friend through the pounding white noise in his head but he could raise not one word of his own. With help, he staggered to the welcome shade of a small desert oak and slumped against its rough trunk.

"You stay here. I'll keep going. Don't worry, I'll be back."

Through eyes slitted against the glare and pain, he watched as the other lad disappeared at a trot into the quivering distance and vaguely wondered, in his dehydrated haze, if that might be the last time he saw his childhood friend.

As the sun began to dip lower towards the horizon, he forced his eyes to open and his legs to carry him, walking in short bursts until the pain in his belly overcame him and again he would lie down in the red sand of his unforgiving homeland.

Walk and lie down. Walk and lie down. His feet found the faint tracks of a road, one of many that criss-crossed this country, and he knew he must follow it. He knew that to succumb to his exhaustion would be fatal but as night fell, he could walk no more.

He lowered his now shivering frame into the warm cradle of the track's aging wheel ruts and closed his eyes.

As his grip on the waking world slipped, his dreams were filled with visions of his tjamu – of following him through the desert, of carrying his spears, of resting his sleepy head against Tjamu's strong neck as he was carried back to camp with the still-warm body of freshly hunted malu balanced on the tjilpi's head.

He woke with a jolt, raising and shaking his head to clear the last wisps from his dreamy vision. There in the distance he saw a flame flickering against the still blackness of the night. Was he still dreaming? Yes, maybe he was dreaming. He closed his eyes again.

"Tjitji! Wake up. Wake up. We are here!"

The voice filtered through the young fella's wavering consciousness and he opened his eyes again.

Swimming before him were two tjilpis, firesticks throwing a halo of light around his saviours as they knelt alongside him.

"Kapi?", he whispered.

"Slowly!" said his rescuer, holding out the precious gift.

But the young fella gulped savagely at the water, and as the liquid hit his churning belly it bounced, spilling bile and the remainder of the green bush tomatoes into the dust like a toxic brown reminder of his youthful ignorance.

The tjilpis exchanged glances.

"Too many bush tomatoes. Make your belly crook and your legs weak. That's a good lesson for you, young fella."

Rousing cheers of celebration greeted their return to camp, and his family wept with relief at his return but it would be a few sunrises yet before the young fella's belly and head stopped reminding him of the near-fatal lessons he had learned.

One day, he would have all the knowledge a man needs to survive in the bush. One day, he would become a man. One day, he would teach his own sons how to survive. One day, he would be able to tell them of the dangers of not listening and learning. One day, he would tell them how his rush to become a man had nearly cost him that opportunity.

One day.

• • • •

Almost half a century later, as Sammy Wilson recounts the story of almost perishing in the bush as a young fella, it's clear the deadly brush with a merciless landscape still resonates deeply.

In that seminal moment in time for the young Sammy there are lessons for many, Anangu and piranpa alike. It is both a reminder and a dire warning – this country can and will nurture the respectful and torture the unprepared.

Once when I was a young fella we set out in the car from Pipalyatjara to go hunting, looking for kangaroo. It was hot in the afternoon at that time – I don't know what season it was. It was just starting to heat up, so maybe around this time of year (October). Mum had gone to Kaltukatjara (Docker River) – can't remember why – maybe funeral or business or something and we were with my grandmother from Amata.

I don't know how old I was that day when we went out in the truck. I wasn't a man yet. I was a kid and I didn't know how much fuel was in the truck and it ran out of fuel. It was an old grey International truck.

We camped the night and then my friend Cisco and I set off walking. We set off at day break and walked and we made it to Puta Puta, where there was kapi; there was a hand pump there. We kept walking, thinking it wasn't too far away and then the sun went there in the sky, maybe two or three o'clock.

But I had been eating too many bush tomatoes as I walked along and that exhausted me, made me sick. I couldn't keep walking. I was really dehydrated. I had no spit. Cisco kept going but I lay down under a tree.

When the sun got lower, I walked again. I knew I had to

keep going, but I'd walk for a little while and then I'd have to lie down again. I would walk, then lie down. Walk then lie down. I was following the road but no one used that road – only once a fortnight for the ration truck. I knew there would be no cars, so I would just lie down in the middle of the road. If there had been a car, I would have been run over.

When it got dark, I was lying asleep. Something woke me up, something like a bite. I've always wondered what it was that bit me and woke me up. And then I saw a light, a flame. It was someone coming with a flare to find me. Two blokes; an old bloke with a firestick and some water, and another bloke who had come to find me because Cisco had made it back to the community and raised the alarm.

When I had the water, I threw up all those bush tomatoes. The old fella said, "That's why you were so weak – eating all those bush tomatoes made you sick and weak."

That's when I learned that you shouldn't eat too many bush tomatoes. I learned the hard way. I was sick for a while after that.

Anyway, that taught me some good lessons about being out in the bush.

• • • •

A visitor to Australia's Red Centre sees first its beauty. A wise visitor also sees its potential danger.

From the time the ancestral beings created this country, Tjukurpa has guided the Anangu along the path to respect for the land, with knowledge passed down through the ages of the proper way to manage it – to work with the land and to live and survive on and from it.

Anangu feel pain and privation just the same as whitefellas. The difference is that, after thousands of years of living and surviving in the harsh desert regions, the Anangu have a far greater tolerance for hardship.

But even with the advent of piranpa tucker, transport and communications, this landscape still demands care and the Uluru family knows more than most just how vital it is to care for the land. There is no better way to do this than through the passing on of knowledge.

In the vast regions of the central and western deserts, the gift of knowledge is the gift of life. For tens of thousands of years, an intimate understanding of the land has sustained the Anangu and, as whitefella history will attest, a lack of understanding or, worse still, to ignore Anangu knowledge, has dire consequences. In a battle between man and Mother Nature, she wins every time. Eventually.

The pages of contemporary history are littered with the corpses of individuals, organisations and endeavours that, through arrogance or ignorance or a lethal combination of both, failed to heed the ancient wisdom of the original inhabitants.

That times have changed is a given, and Anangu too have embraced many of those changes, but the Uluru family still holds fast if not to the practice of traditional ways in everyday life then certainly to the passing on of that knowledge as a sacred inheritance for coming generations.

It's a classic "need to know" basis. Because knowledge IS sacred and they helped me to understand, through teaching me different aspects of Tjukurpa, just how sacred knowledge is and how sacred language is.

You cannot survive in this country without intimate knowledge of the country – of plants, of water, of the right way to use things, what not to use, what you can and can't eat and how things change. Without that understanding, you won't survive in this country, at least in the traditional way.

Through teaching me their culture, their knowledge, they actually taught me how special knowledge is not just for Anangu but for all humanity, for every culture. They were teaching me concepts that were different to what I knew and that taught me that within language and Tjukurpa, stories of the country from the country, that's the knowledge of life. I don't think you can get any bigger than that for humanity.[1]

I had the luxury during my time with the Uluru family of not having to worry about survival in this beautiful but unforgiving landscape and therefore did not necessarily have that vital need for traditional knowledge. But, mindful of the value of fostering greater understanding in the wider community, the family happily offered fascinating snippets of information about learning the old ways, proper ways, and of growing up at a time when malu-wipu (kangaroo tail) came from the bush not the supermarket.

Reggie:

I remember the time when malu wipu came from malu, not from the freezer at the shop. Out bush when we caught a kangaroo we would eat the tail straight after cooking but now we put salt on it.

We would bury the food, the meat, in the ground to cook and cover it with grasses afterwards to keep it cool. The meat would keep nicely and it was good because it could make it look like you had nothing, but there it was all under the ground – malu wipa and everything. You could store a lot like that and it would keep it fresh. Perentie lizard, kangaroo – everything we could keep like this and it wouldn't go off.

Sometimes people sang songs to make the kids happy while gathering and preparing food. The men would hunt for the meat and the women would get the other tucker.

To make a good spear, you have to find good wood. And you have to have been able to go out and hunt a kangaroo to get the sinew from the kangaroo and then get the right head for that spear and then bind the head of the spear to the wood using the sinew. With certain types of spinifex grass, you beat it and collect the crystallised sap that comes out then you heat it over the fire to make resin – that is called kiti and it is used to stick things together. It's used to hold stone knives in place; spearheads and that sort of thing. I can show you how to make kiti. When your spear is made, you're ready then in the afternoon to go out hunting.

That's what I want our young fellas to learn out on their homelands. Teach them that before they were born, this is how people used to get their food – they would go out and hunt with the spears they made.

I was good with a spear but it's a hard thing to do to sneak up on malu without them being alerted to your presence. I couldn't do it well, but my brother Cassidy, he was better. He could sneak up on a kangaroo because he could make this noise: tch, tch, tch… You have to be able to make this noise because that's what a mother kangaroo does to signal her young that there's danger. Cassidy was very good at sneaking up on them. He used to show tourists how he would sneak up. He would get down low and go very carefully then he would freeze, waiting for the kangaroo to be distracted again, then he'd move on slowly then freeze, move closer then freeze… that's how he used to sneak up on the kangaroo. You have to go reeeeallly slowly. It takes a lot of patience. You have to keep moving forward when you see that they're distracted, like while they're digging in the sand or eating, then you move closer and closer until you're sure that you're not going to miss when you throw your spear.

You have to be able to spear them here in the chest – in the heart. When you speared the kangaroo and killed him, you would build a fire and cook it up quite close by.

Other people who weren't with the hunter (back at the camp) would think, "Hmm…where's that hunter? Maybe he's got one?" and so they would look out for the signs and would see the smoke, "See that, there's a fire!" and the kids in particular would go "Hey, let's go get some kangaroo meat!" and they'd run off towards the fire. Then they would sit around and wait until the hunter said it was okay to eat.

Kangaroos can be dangerous. They can fight back with

their front paws and they can fight with their tails too. And they can also bite. They will grab you in a headlock and they will bite you on your head or face.

I've been bitten by a kangaroo, when I was a young teenager at Mimili. I got too close and it was an aggressive kangaroo and it grabbed me. That's what they do – they grab you and hold onto you and they'll try to kick you with their back legs as well as bite you. Very dangerous.

But we ended up eating that kangaroo.

That is why once you spear the kangaroo, you always hit it on the back of the neck with a piece of wood to make sure it's dead. But it grabbed me this time. I was glad there was another young fella with me and he came and hit the kangaroo on the head and killed it. Then we ate him.

Ngintaka (perentie lizard) can bite you too. It has teeth as sharp as a knife and it can bite you badly. Ngintaka can get quite aggressive too, it can be like mamu (evil spirit). It can see you nearby and suddenly turn on you and chase you. It's very frightening and you have to run fast. Even if you spear him, he can still chase you until you are quite exhausted and you have to spear him again. You have to spear it in the head to kill it. You definitely shouldn't climb a tree because he will chase you up the tree and then you are in big trouble because you are trapped. It's really bad being chased by a ngintaka.

Maybe the reason it's aggressive is that it has a memory in its head of being attacked by someone in the past. It might recognise you. It might remember that you were that one who tried to stone it once before. It might think, "That's the fella who tried to get me, so I'm going to get him this time!" Even though it mightn't actually have been you – he would just see a man and think, "A man hit me before!" so he'll charge at you. And you gotta run! You have to be able to try to find something as you run – something to turn around and throw at him.

If that's happened and you've killed him, you can't just

leave him. You have to hang him up. Put him up in a tree. You don't eat him, no. Because he's rama (mad). He's wrong way, that one. So you hang him up in a tree. If you eat him, you might get that wrong way too.

A tjitji might be there and say, "Hey Dad – that's a good ngintaka, good feed!" but the father will say "No, no – we can't eat him!" A way to explain it – because the child might be upset that you're leaving good food behind – is to say that no, that ngintaka he's too skinny. Tell him he's no good.

There is a little black monitor lizard called nyintjiri – he's no good to eat either. We see them over at the rock. You can't eat them. Make you sick. He has a black head and he lives in the rocks.

Liru, he's a poisonous snake. He will come around looking for fruit plants. If people are collecting bush tucker and fruit without thinking about the liru, it might be lying in wait for them. It might be thinking "I'll just wait here and maybe a tjitji will come along and I'll just be waiting for that tjitji."

The father would always be keeping an eye out – saying, "Hey, wait a minute and watch out for snakes. Hold back!" – and then the father would check to make sure there were no snakes in the area before letting the children run around to collect bush tucker.

The adults would always be sure to check out the area and make sure it is clear of liru before allowing the children near the area. That is really important because if you get bitten you don't have long to live. It's really poisonous and the poison is very fast. You will die quickly if you get bitten and you don't get the poison out straight away. Say, if you were bitten here on the wrist, a ngangkari (traditional healer) would suck out the poison.* But you had to get to the ngangkari fast.

It is important to warn tjitji about snakes. If you're asleep, a snake might come up and wrap around your head and lick the moisture from your nostrils. It's happened to me. I woke up to see the tracks right next to me.

We always warn kids about snake danger. Have to teach them early to be fearful in case they try to play with it.

Sometimes if you catch a liru and kill it, you hang it up on the fence so that other snakes will smell it and avoid the area.

We were at Mimili when I was a tjitji and one time when the adults had all gone out hunting, all the tjitji were left behind. There was a snake on the ground near an ili (fig) tree. We were collecting the figs and we didn't check for liru, so we didn't see it. One kid was bitten and lost their life. I was nearly speared by my dad when he came home. That was the typical punishment for if you did something wrong. He said, "You didn't care for the other kids carefully enough and that's why that happened – that's why that tjitji died."

I was bitten on the thigh by a snake once when I was a small child at Amaroona near where I was born, but I was treated by a ngangkari and I was okay. There were no white doctors in those days.

That was okay because, wiya, we never got sick. If someone would get sick you would seek out a ngangkari and the bush doctor would often find that the sick person's spirit was displaced (makes a motion of rubbing his stomach) and the ngangkari would massage the spirit back into its proper place.

Sometimes if someone became ill and they left it too long to seek out a traditional healer, they might die. Sometimes the traditional healer does come but might find out they're too late and the person is very close to dying. People would then go into mourning.

The person might have become sick from eating something they shouldn't eat. Sometimes there might be some kind of insect that might be in an edible fruit that will make you sick if you eat it, even though the fruit is okay, the insect isn't. That's why it's so important for us to educate people, children especially, about what is safe to eat and what's not safe to eat.

We have lots of different species of bush tucker and lots

of different names for them. We have quandong and figs and bush tomatoes – we call bush tomatoes wiriny-wirinypa; some people call it the desert raisin. We also dig at a special kind of tree for maku (witchetty grubs) and other tucker. Lots of bush tucker if you know where to find it and what is good and what is not and when to eat it so it won't make you sick.

I remember being at Mimili with my father. I remember Andrew, my brother. We were always with our dad and we were always very happy to be with him, going hunting.

This is what you did with your children in those days – they would travel with you. You did everything with your tjitji. They would go everywhere with you. You always were wangkara wangkapai (talking to them) and telling them things they need to know.

In the 1930s, after contact with piranpa began in earnest, Anangu were introduced to the strange and convenient whitefella tucker on which they would come to rely, by both design and necessity.

What woman wouldn't choose a bag of ready-ground white flour over eight hours of backbreaking work to gather, grind and prepare a meagre crop of grass seeds for cooking? Who among us could resist the sweet addiction of that first taste of sugar? And when introduced livestock began to thin the once bountiful herds of native fauna, and when Anangu were fenced off from traditional hunting grounds, what choice but to accept the offering of the whitefella's rations?

During the depression, many white men made their way into the central desert in search of dingo scalps for which the government was paying a bounty. These doggers, as they became known, began to exchange whitefella food (flour, tinned meat, sugar and the like) for the scalps of native dogs gathered by the Anangu.

So began the journey towards disease and diabetes for these trusting indigenous communities. It's a scourge of which the older members of the Uluru family are acutely aware, and time and again our discussions around traditional ways turn to a lament for healthier times. For Anangu elders, the conundrum is painful. Like whitefella medicines, which have been both a blessing and a curse according to some elders, the introduction of sugar, tobacco and alcohol in particular have had far reaching consequences down through the generations. It helps little to explain that the same is true for modern generations of piranpa.

> When I was growing up there weren't all these different things going on – we didn't have all the harmful things that affect Anangu now. None of this – sugar, cigarettes, no processed food – no store-bought food. We ate our native food, off the country. We had the grasses for flour and the animals for meat. No sugar. Sugar has been very bad.
>
> I remember all the family members – the extended family were really healthy and happy. They never suffered from diabetes, wiya. No-one got sick. People just died of old age. We didn't have modern medicines – didn't need them. We just used bush medicine, things like eremophila** for colds or sore throats or things like that.[2]

Not only does the older generation of Uluru family lament the loss of a healthy lifestyle for Anangu, they also keenly feel the impact of modern times and ways on the opportunity to bond with and teach younger generations in the traditional "proper way". Again, this is true for humanity as a whole as society changes, but that loss is all the more painful for a people whose culture, language and family lore were never written down. That theirs is an oral history makes it all the more vulnerable.

Sammy:

I remember my Tjamu, Paddy Uluru. He was my grandfather. He was tall and skinny. He was a quiet man.

He used to take me out bush with him when he went out to cut punu (wood) to make boomerangs. Then he would tell me to wait and he'd just disappear. I'd sit and wait under a tree and he would come back with a kangaroo.

Tjamu Uluru taught me how to make a spear, how to use the spear too. He used to make spears at the home camp, but he always went out bush to make boomerangs. Later we had rifles.

I used to get very tired, so when it was time to come home, Tjamu Uluru would put the hunt, malu or whatever, on his head, and he'd lift me up onto his back and I'd carry his boomerangs. He'd carry me home like that – tired one.

I grew up when things were more free. When I was young, I used to walk around the bush with a shanghai – I'd hunt rabbits and lizards and all kinds of things.

I would like to see the young fellas still going out and walking around the homelands. It's no good for people to sit down in the communities all the time. They need to get out and get to know their homelands. There needs to be investment into homelands and into teaching the younger people about their homelands.

The water is still out there, so you can get water and now there are bores out there that have been sunk. But there's nothing else out there that people will go out there for so it would be nice to develop something else out there to encourage them to go out there into the bush – something like what we've done at Patji (where Sammy often takes tourists as part of his Uluru Family Tours operation).

If Anangu go out bush, the young people work for the old people – the young ones do all the work because it's the old ones who are teaching them. But now, all the old people are in aged care facilities, being looked after by the system. They are looked after physically but they're not out on country or visiting their homelands any more. That's why I call it gaol.

Patji is an important place for us. What we do there is go to sit down. Yes, it's a sacred place. Some I can tell you but some I can't tell you. It's part of men's business – I can't tell you.*** Anangu were living there long time. But I can tell you about the country – I can tell you how we follow the water, follow the plants, follow the Tjukurpa. Tjukurpa and stories are our inheritance. They are very important.

I have four sons. Three live here. When we go out hunting, out on country, I show them the old ways. Show them how to hunt and how to cook – show them traditional way. There are different stories for different children. "This is your story and this is your story." Once they are men, that's when I know they are able to keep those stories. Tjamu (grandfather), uncles – they tell the stories.

Bush boys have to stay out in the bush for that time. Bush boys – this is like a training camp, away from the main camp. They have to stay out there – they still get a feed and the things they need, but they're not allowed to come to the main camp. They are out there to learn about hunting and whatever else they need to know.

Old men might come and visit – all the tjilpis and tjamus– might come and show the wati how to make boomerangs and things like that. Tell them about things they need to know.

I was lucky during my bush camp time I had a car so I could go further out into the bush. Sometimes we'd get the younger fellas, who weren't secluded, and get them to go back to town and get us some supplies because we only had the basics – tea-leaves, sugar. We'd make little day trips – go out and hunt a malu and then go to the waterhole and swim. Then we'd make a big fire at the bush camp and cook up the malu we'd hunted.

It was a time when you would learn your country – learn about where all the waterholes are and all the different sites. All the things you need to know. I still know all these things. I've also taken young fellas out and been part of their education. These days it's a bit different, though.

These days, a lot is different. Conscious of just how fragile and vulnerable is the environment and complex ecosystems of the central desert regions, whitefella authorities are again turning to the

Sammy Wilson (T'jama Uluru), Mutitjulu 2016. *Photo: Jen Cowley*

Anangu for knowledge of ancient practices for caring for the land. Of particular interest and importance is the use of fire in protecting and managing the environment. Fires and burning have been a part of the Anangu and Tjukurpa way of land management for tens of thousands of years. The burning of country began with creation beings, with Lungkata (the blue-tongue lizard ancestral being) burning the tjanpi (spinifex) as he made his journey across the land to Uluru from the north.

The traditional use of fire was not just for cooking or for warmth or even as a means of communication. It was also an integral part of Tjukurpa's decree about caring for and managing the land from which Anangu needed to survive. An intricate knowledge of the way the land and its flora and fauna responded to fire, and of the way fire in turn behaved in certain areas, was vital.

Traditional burning in the Uluru region ceased with the removal of Anangu during the early twentieth century. Piranpa considered fire dangerous so actively stopped Anangu burning in the traditional way. Throughout the 1940s, rainfall was plentiful across the region and plant life flourished but in 1950 a massive fire, fuelled by that overabundance of growth, wiped out about a third of the Uluru-Kata Tjuta National Park's vegetation. That pattern was repeated over and over and in 1976, two fires destroyed some 76 per cent of the park.[4]

In a bid to break the cycle and to prevent further damage to the diversity of the area's vegetation, the management of the park turned to the Anangu for help, developing a system of patch-burning that is still used and overseen by traditional owners.

While this is a welcome practice, its effectiveness has been irreversibly diluted by other significant changes to Anangu life. There has been an immense social cost for Anangu from the interruption to traditional methods of fire management, in that families have strong fire-lines similar to story- or song-lines. These family fire-lines are based on intimate and minutely specific acquaintance of their particular country, built on knowledge gained while literally walking country, gathering intricate details of the environment, its flora and fauna and idiosyncrasies as the Anangu walked back and forth. They knew exactly where and when and how to burn, how it would affect the plants and animals, how the fire would behave, when and where it would burn itself out and, importantly, when rain would come.

Anangu now do not regularly walk this country as they did in the old days, so much of that intricate knowledge is held only by the elders and only then by instinct because, like all indigenous cultural practice, it was never written down. It was an oral knowledge, only to be passed on through to coming generations as they too walked their country. Now, authorities (including many Anangu) are fearful of upsetting Tjukurpa (traditional law, song-lines, story-lines) by burning without this specific knowledge. This makes back-burning or hazard reduction a very tricky business indeed. As a result, when a fire does start, which can happen in any number of ways, it will often burn a much greater area than it would have had it been controlled burning by traditional Anangu with intimate knowledge of their specific family-fire-lines.

There is much to be learned from Anangu in terms of environmental practice and fortunately this truth is being acknowledged, accepted and adopted widely – better late than never. Sammy speaks of the passing on of culture as "the gift of knowledge". That gift from traditional indigenous culture is offered willingly. Our challenge is to receive it.

• • • •

* *While the attention of a traditional healer for snake bite is widely regarded by traditional Anangu, modern medical professionals do not recommend this method of treatment. Identification of venomous snakes can be made from venom present on clothing or the skin using a so called 'venom detection' kit. If you are bitten by a snake, seek medical attention immediately and do not wash or suck the bite or discard clothing. A pressure immobilisation bandage is recommended for anyone bitten by a venomous snake. This involves firmly bandaging the area of the body involved, such as the arm or leg, and keeping the person calm and still until medical help arrives. (www.healthdirect.gov.au)*

** Eremophila/s — *Many traditional medicines and remedies can be found in the central desert region, but the most prized is eremophila, which is widely referred to as "bush medicine" amongst Anangu and features widely in artworks from the APY and NPY lands, both traditional and contemporary. The leaves from the native bush are collected (almost always by women) then ground and boiled. The resin this elicits is mixed with oil or fat to make an ointment. In more traditional times, the women would use emu fat, but today the ubiquitous olive oil or wax does the job. The resulting ointment is good for all kinds of remedies, particularly in helping to heal wounds and bites and skin irritations. It also acts as an effective and natural insect repellent and the powdered version can be put directly onto the chest to help ease congestion. The leaves of the eremophila bush can also be boiled with the inhalation of the steam assisting with the easing of chest complaints. This versatile eremophila can also help with stomach upsets. Bush medicine is an important part of traditional life for Anangu and these days, a trip out on country to collect these precious leaves is a treat in itself.*

*** As explained elsewhere in this account of the Uluru family's history, the sharing of knowledge and information is fraught for Anangu elders, particularly the discussion of "men's business" with a woman (Anangu or otherwise). The Uluru family men are gentle but firm with their explanations of why it is impossible to discuss certain things, and it is to their credit that they have learned to give context and general information without breaking sacred law. I also had to learn how to accept these explanations and to be grateful to receive them. That they will never break that sacred code both sates my curiosity and strengthens my deep admiration.

1. Interview at Mutitjulu (October 2017) with Kate Vickers, a ranger with Uluru-Kata Tjuta National Parks who worked with the Uluru family and Anangu Tours. Her insights are reproduced with permission.
2. Alan Wilson – from interview conducted at Mutitjulu 2016
3. Tjintu Tjuta Kaltukatjarala (Days in Docker River); J.Cowley, 2016; Kungka Kutjara Aboriginal Corporation.
4. Uluru-Kata Tjuta National Park fact sheet, Parks Australia, 2015

CHAPTER 11

"A name is just for paper"

At well over six foot in the old scale and with an ample bulk to match, Sammy Wilson cuts an imposing figure by any measure but it is his acutely observant demeanour that commands attention.

He is quick to laugh, and to see his frame shudder with mirth is an infectious sight to behold, but he is equally quick to call out insincerity and he suffers no fools. He tells it like it is and his disarming honesty can be at once refreshing and terrifying. He has seen and heard far too much to take anything he sees or hears at face value.

As "head" of the Uluru family, if such a thing exists beyond a whitefella label, and as chairperson of the Uluru-Kata Tjuta Board of Management, Sammy Wilson bears a great responsibility that comes with his Anangu name. As a young fella, the name sat uncomfortably. Now, as he shoulders that weight every day, he understands and welcomes its inalienable bond to family, to country, to Tjukurpa. He IS Uluru and nothing can change that. "A name is just for paper."

Some of my ancestors were born in Scotland, but that's not my place. I wasn't born in hospital, I was born right here across the road there, north of Indulkana on a station called DeRose Hill.

My mum was Nellie Uluru, daughter of Paddy Uluru from his first wife. She was born on Yankunytjatjara country and my stepfather, Peter Wilson, was born on Pitjantjatjara country. I took his name when my mother met him at Kulgera. She was promised to him because they were right way. So then she married him and I went with them out west – out to Wingellina.

Paddy Uluru was my Tjamu. In this way, I am older brother to what whitefellas would call my cousins. That's the way it works. Reggie and Cassidy Uluru are my uncles. I was born emu dreaming, same as Reggie. My country is here, his country is there but we are both emu dreaming.

They used to call me Uluru because they knew I was Uluru's grandson. That's the name they used. I was Tjama Uluru. I got my name in Amata. Because the whitefellas couldn't understand "Tjama", they gave me the name Sam. Then it became Sammy. Sammy Wilson – Wilson after my stepfather.

My Anangu name is Tjama. I would prefer to be called Tjama – Anangu call me Tjama. But everyone knows me as Sammy. My last name is Uluru, but it can be difficult. I got really stressed out when I went to school at Amata because I saw that everyone else had a long name and my name was just short – Sam. So I thought, okay, I can be Sammy.

That was okay and then they said, well, what's your surname? I had no idea what they were talking about so I ran home, ran away from school.

My mum took me back and we found out what they were trying to ask. They were trying to find out my second name. My mum's second name was Uluru, but I already knew about the rock and I thought it was a bit strange so I didn't want that name. I'd heard all these stories about this great big rock. I remember seeing it for the first time. When I was younger I had no idea. I remember hearing about Cassidy's reaction when he first saw it, he was frightened and ran away.

Even now, people come here and they are intimidated by the rock, they find it a bit overwhelming somehow. So that's why I didn't want to be called Uluru. They were trying to get me to use that name but I didn't want to know about it. So then they came up with the idea of using my stepfather's name – Wilson – and I was happy with that. Perhaps I should have kept that name, Tjama Uluru, but at the time I was thinking about how children tease each other, that happens across all communities. I didn't want them to be able to tease me about being called Uluru.

I am Uluru, I am Anangu. A name can't change that. A name is just for paper.

Sammy's life until now has been a colourful, if sometimes painful, blend of traditional Anangu ways in a contemporary whitefella world. He is deeply committed to Tjukurpa and culture but has managed, through agonising trial and tormenting error, to find a balance on what he has described as the highway of life for Anangu – there are white lines and signs for guidance, but it's important to always keep the tyres on the black road.

When I was a tjitji, we were camped bush-style at Ronald's Well; in wiltjas (bush shelters) near Mimili before there was a community there, before the station. That was in the 1960s. Before I was a teenager. With Tjamu Uluru, we went from Mimili to Ronald's Well – its name is Unkanpalangu – there was kapi there. Cassidy and Reggie were at Mimili at that time. Then they took me back to DeRose Hill Station.

I used to hang out with the teenage boys in their bush camp when they were separated from the rest of the mob, while they were waiting for their men's ceremonies. Sometimes I would have to go back home in the middle of the night from those camps. We didn't think about age or years when we were becoming men – there wasn't a certain age. We just became men.

There was no school in Mimili, but I went to school in Indulkana, Amata, Docker River, Fregon, Ernabella… I didn't sit down in one place and go to school. Our family travelled all around the place. If something happened over here, then we'd have to go there and do that thing; if something else happened over there, then we needed to go there. Always something going on.

We all moved a lot, not sitting down in one house like we do now. My mum was Yangkutatjara, my stepfather was Pitjantjatjara – she came from the east and he came from the west but we travelled all across that country, so I am true man from NPY lands.

Sometimes we'd walk, sometimes in a motorcar. We walked when the motorcar broke down. We would just camp out in the bush. One time the car broke down and we couldn't get to Mulga Park so we made a shelter and just waited it out. We walked to Mulga Park after the rain. There were lots of people camping at Mulga Park then.

One time I walked from Nyapari to Pipalyatjara – same thing, car broke down. We were shifting camp from Nyapari to Kanpi because it was too windy. The car broke down so we started walking with all our things. The mail truck came along, carrying rations and supplies and mail, so we took advantage of that truck to put our blankets and tents and things on but there was no room for us with all the other supplies on the truck, so we walked. The bloke said, "I can carry this, but I can't carry you." It was after rain, so there was plenty of water along the way. It took us a few days. There were people camping at Pipalyatjara and some were at Puta Puta – near the border of South Australia – so we were heading there to see them.

I was in Yalata in the late 1970s and I came back to Mimili in about 1980. Unfortunately, I was a petrol sniffer. I learned to sniff petrol in Amata. When you sniff petrol, you close your eyes and you lie down like you're asleep and you see things. You hallucinate. You see things coming at you, like big snakes crawling towards you and things like that. But no one else can see these things, just you. It's scary.

I did that for some time in the '70s – too long. That's how I wound up in Yalata community. Then they put me into the stock camp to try to get me off the petrol sniffing. That's how I got off the petrol – I stopped sniffing and started working. That was good for a while. Then I started hanging around with marijuana people. That lasted until the late '80s but then I gave up smoking marijuana because of the birth of my daughter. Now, I tell young people don't do it. Don't sniff petrol. Don't smoke marijuana. I still carry that with me, even though I gave up a long time ago.

My life really changed when I came to Mutitjulu to live. Working and having a family helped me to get off the petrol and off the marijuana. Sometimes I'd go to courses to help me get skills. I realised that working was better. I felt better inside myself. What I'm telling you now is that it takes a long time to get off it but it takes even longer time to get over it. The damage stays with you. So it's important to me now to say something to young people.

Communication, as in any society, has been key to the maintenance of Anangu society for thousands of years, particularly given its almost exclusively oral nature. The passing of knowledge, the telling of stories, the conferral of Tjukurpa and even the structure of day-to-day life – all these have assured survival for Anangu in an otherwise unforgiving landscape. For countless generations, this structure guided what to do, when, how and why to do it and where and with whom. So the dilution and fracturing of that ancient structure of communication, through the natural attrition wrought by modern methods, has been among the most difficult of transitions for Anangu.

Anangu have always been here. The government system (Anangu) if you want to put it in whitefella way, was run by the early morning talking, like broadcasting – the elders calling out across the camp in the morning. This is called alpiri. From this, the people would know what they had to do each day. As everyone was just stirring, the older men, the elders would be calling out their news for the morning. They would call out across the camp to tell everyone what the plan for the day was; what was going to happen and what needed to happen. Then another elder might call out from the other side of the camp, or from a nearby camp with his news and that's how the day was planned.

They might be planning whether to shift camp that day or which way they were going to hunt for malu; sometimes they might have heard news that there's some kind of sickness or poisoning. The ngangkaris' (traditional healers') spirits might have travelled during the night and learned about something going wrong. The ngangkari are those who can see and hear the spirit world and can sense and predict danger coming. They can see if someone is sending something or some danger being sent that the people need to protect themselves from.

The word will go out, "Hey, you'd better stay close to your fires – stay warm so you don't get sick". Mamu (bad spirit) will bring illness, a physical illness. It will make pika (fight) with your body – a disease of the spirit that causes you to fight.

Marriages were also arranged in that way, through those morning alpiri from the elders. They might be calling out to another campfire, between family groups, that there was a kungka that is in the right marriage arrangement for you. That would be a discussion between the senior men of the camp, not with the women. There would be a wati waiting, and an old man might say, "My granddaughter is over there and she's right way for him to marry".

When I was a tjitji, I remember waking up and wondering if the old men were having a fight, but no, they were just talking and doing their business and arranging business for the day. Nowadays, you can't do that because everyone is in their houses – so you can't plan for the day like they used to.

Old habits die hard around these parts. While the mercury of a Mutitjulu summer can climb well past the comfortable point, you will rarely find the door to Sammy's modern-style house open. Even when the temperature nudges past the old century mark, the door remains shut against any breeze that might give relief.

Despite growing up in the bush, where sleep came under a canopy of stars with no doors between the slumbering world and the wide-open desert, Sammy now closes his eyes for sleep only when the door to his house is firmly shut against the world. Why? Because someone might come to the door, uninvited and possibly unwelcome. When you're out in the bush, you can hear danger approaching. You can feel the change in the breeze, sense the shift in the landscape. Behind walls, you can't hear peril's footfall or feel menace on the wind. There is no subtle warning of approaching danger.

In this modern world, so far removed in so many ways from the one he knew as a tjitji, there are new threats, new risks to Tjukurpa.

In this new world, Sammy Wilson's mind and heart are open, but that door – like the door to some aspects of Tjukurpa – stays shut.

CHAPTER 12

"Welcome to my home"

It is an unsettling irony that the very existence and universally powerful majesty of Uluru and Kata Tjuta, the spiritual headquarters for Anangu and the Uluru family, would in effect help to bring about such a tragic period in their history.

Had Uluru and Kata Tjuta been unremarkable geographical features, their ancient secrets hidden from view by terrestrial ordinariness, the contemporary Anangu story might have been very different.

That they are both such special places is a sacred blessing for Anangu, but the interest and curiosity these iconic features engender from the outside world has been in equal measure a curse in many ways. And yet, in a perverse way, the outside world's fascination with Uluru and Kata Tjuta presents an opportunity to maintain Anangu culture.

This is something the Uluru family understands fully. From the moment Paddy returned from exile to find whitefellas desecrating the deep sacredness of the rock, the die was cast. He knew then that only through appropriately guiding piranpa in the ways of Tjukurpa and Anangu culture would there be any hope of preserving both. He passed that understanding, along with knowledge of Tjukurpa and culture, to his descendants who have taken that baton in the quest to educate and inform the outside world so as to help preserve that which is most sacred.

That Uluru and Kata Tjuta have the ability to take the first-time visitor's breath away is by no means new, to either Anangu or piranpa.

Thirty-one-year-old English-born explorer William Christie Gosse saw the rock, the first whitefella to do so, in 1873.* His diary notes from July 19, although relatively perfunctory, hint at the wonder of that first glimpse. As he crossed "the wretched country" the intrepid Gosse saw what he believed to be a hill rising from the desert in the distance. As he drew closer he saw, to what he described as his "astonishment", that it was in fact "one immense rock rising abruptly from the plain".[1]

In bare feet and with great difficulty, Gosse managed to climb what he named Ayers Rock. His were the first of many millions of whitefella feet that would follow.

But Anangu too tell of amazement at their first glimpse of Uluru. There is a word, kakulyarani, that approximates the English expression of shock and awe. It is used by many to describe their reaction to seeing the rock for the first time, including Cassidy who recalls his initial shock as a seven- or eight-year-old, saying he was at first frightened by the sight of the gargantuan Uluru.

Given it has stood sentry over the central desert and its people since the dawn of time, Uluru's trajectory into the tourism space has been remarkably steep.

Following its discovery by whitefellas in the late nineteenth century, it remained relatively untouched thanks to the surrounding region being deemed too inhospitable to sustain the pastoral expansion the explorers were seeking on behalf of the colony.

In the ensuing three decades or so, piranpa came only in a trickle. Save for a few hardy souls in the shape of surveyors, prospectors and scientists, the region was considered unworthy of the effort given its apparent lack of pastoral potential and resources.

That inadvertent inoculation against wholesale piranpa invasion would not last forever, though, and from the early 1900s, exploration began to pick up speed and by the beginning of the 1930s the tourist bug had bitten.

In the 1920s, the governments of South Australia, Western Australia and the Commonwealth made the arguably well-intentioned move to set aside an area called the Petermann Aboriginal Reserve, which included Uluru and Kata Tjuta. The idea was to provide an area for the protection of the nomadic inhabitants of the vast central desert regions who had essentially no contact whatsoever with whitefellas, but a cynic might suggest the authorities of the day saw the land as devoid of resources and therefore of no value anyway.

White visitors continued to beat a path to Uluru and Kata Tjuta, and in 1948 the first road suitable for vehicles was built in response to growing curiosity. Tour buses began to roll in during the early 1950s and in 1951 an application was made to the government to allow tourist flights to Uluru. Basic tourist facilities soon followed.

In 1954 a group of students from Knox Grammar School in Sydney visited Uluru on a school excursion. Newsreel images and commentary from the time are cringeworthy, showing images of "station blacks" and offering that "they mightn't look it, but they're nearly civilised…" while pointing out that "the wild blacks go completely naked…"

In 1958, as pressure from tourism operators mounted, the government responded by excising 132,000 hectares from the reserve to become a national park including, of course, the jewels in the central Australian tourism crown, Uluru and Kata Tjuta. Without consultation or consideration for Anangu, the area became the Ayers Rock-Mount Olga National Park, to be managed by the Northern Territory Reserves Board.

The first ranger for the park was Bill Harney who eventually worked closely and was well regarded by the Uluru family and wider Anangu society, but was initially unwelcoming of their presence.

Reggie recalls Harney's reaction to his father Paddy's return from Mimili:

> He wasn't very welcoming. He said "What are you doing here? This is not your country." And my father said, "No, I AM Uluru. This is my country."

Cassidy too recalls an overtly cool reception:

> I remember when I was little, I was kicked out of the tourist area at Uluru. They didn't want me playing around where the tourists were.
>
> That used to happen quite a bit.

Other family members recount that in the early days there were complaints from tourists about Aboriginal people, "lazy blacks", intruding on their holiday experience, so Anangu were often hunted away from Uluru and Kata Tjuta.

The ranger's discomfort would likely have been compounded by Paddy's distress at seeing white tourists desecrating the many sacred sites around Uluru and Kata Tjuta. Paddy's anguish again drove him away to Mimili, but he soon realised the wholesale violation would only be minimised by an effort to educate the piranpa ranger and those he knew would follow. By now aware that the word of Anangu would mostly fall on the deaf ears of piranpa authorities, Paddy enlisted the help of some sympathetic white people who had been urging him to clarify the most sacred sites of Uluru and Kata Tjuta before they were forever obliterated by the swelling wave of tourism. So he again returned, this time with assistance and the intention of guiding the ranger and tourist operators as to which sites were forbidden by Tjukurpa to visitors.

By the 1960s, hand-made artefacts had begun to emerge as a commodity, with Anangu making and selling mementos to the tourists. This was also around the time the government ceased payments to pastoralists for the rations given to Aboriginal people living on stations. Most of the station owners promptly stopped distributing the provisions on which many Anangu families had come to rely. Many went bush again to try to live off the land but too much had changed, not the least of which was the growing scarcity of native animals.

As a consequence, Anangu became increasingly subservient to tourism.[2]

By the time the '70s rolled around, Ayers Rock and The Olgas had become firmly embedded in the Australian tourism landscape. In 1972, the Ininti Store was established as an Aboriginal enterprise, on a lease arrangement with the park entity, to offer services and supplies to visitors and became the nucleus of a permanent Anangu community within what was then the national park.[3]

The Aboriginal Land Rights (Northern Territory) Act of 1976

and the establishment of the Central Land Council meant Anangu finally began to have at least a modicum of say, and in 1984, nearly ten years after the environmental impact of tourist facilities in the park were identified, the resort "town" of Yulara was officially opened 15 kilometres from Uluru to coincide with the removal of all accommodation in the park itself.

The following year, in 1985, the management of the park was granted to the traditional owners through the Uluru Kata Tjuta Aboriginal Land Trust at a momentous occasion that has come to be widely known as "hand back".

Paddy didn't live to see the culmination of the efforts he had begun way back on that day of his return to Uluru. He died in 1979 but his family has kept flame burning and his grandson Sammy Wilson – Tjama Uluru – is, at the time of writing, the chairman of the Uluru Kata-Tjuta Aboriginal Land Trust.

By necessity, tourism has been a significant part of the Uluru family story, underscored and guided, as always, by Tjukurpa.

Reggie:

Paddy, my father, was here at Uluru and they used to do inma (traditional dances) for the tourists. They would put a hat out and the tourists would put money into the hat. No idea where that money ended up – should have put it in the bank.

In the early days we used to take the tourists around the rock and we would tell them some of the stories, like the blue-tongue lizard story and the mala story and we would do inma for them. Only the public things, not the sacred stuff.

There were lots of tourists. That was the days before the chain. I remember someone falling from the rock in those days, before they had the chain there. The tourists are still coming here. They still want to see Uluru. They come from a long way away, from overseas even, to visit. All those people who came before have taken their photos back and shown their families and friends and after a while, those people say "Okay, I want to go and see it for myself now." So that tradition of visiting keeps going.

*Anangu elder*** :**

In the early days, we would do dances for the tourists and we would put a hat out and people would throw money in the hat. The young kids would do the dancing. With the money tourists gave us for dancing, we bought a blue bus and we used that for travelling.

This was back in the days when the tourists and Anangu were all in the same place, so if Anangu were sitting around carving then the tourists would be standing around watching. They weren't really staring – they would say "hello", "good morning" – they were generally friendly and happy to meet us. They'd often ask us "Is this how you live?" and we'd say yes, we live like this and every day there's more of you coming to see us.

When we'd talk to tourists, they'd ask us questions. So we'd ask them questions to square them back. We'd say, "We're from here – where are you from?"

They came to see Aboriginal country. We'd tell them that it's not just here that Aboriginal people live, there are Aboriginal people all over the place – in Alice Springs, in Adelaide. All across Australia there are people like us. They all seemed to have the impression that this is the one point for Aboriginal people – they think that because Uluru is so famous.

In the 1990s, the family was instrumental in establishing and running Anangu Tours, an operation staffed almost exclusively by Anangu and unique in its focus on educating as well as entertaining tourists.

The halcyon Anangu Tours days are some of the most fondly remembered by the Uluru family, which was pivotal to the business. Of particular importance to the success of the enterprise was Andrew

Uluru, brother to Reggie and Cassidy, who is remembered as "the glue that held it all together".

Andrew, who died from cancer in the early 2000s and is buried next to his father Paddy at Mutitjulu cemetery, was a quieter style of man to his brothers, less charismatic but no less clever in his adaptation to the business of tourism or skilled in his understanding of people. While their innate charisma meant his brothers drew the higher profile, Andrew was a solid stayer, reliable and consistent.

According to those who worked closely with Andrew, there was a shrewdness behind his quiet demeanour. He quickly adapted his patter to tourists to reflect his equally quick learning about the ways of whitefellas. He was able to evolve his connection with other cultures so as to offer a unique and meaningful experience for visitors interested in his own.

Wiry of build, like Cassidy, and always sporting a hat, like Reggie, Andrew neither married nor had children but was loved and respected by his family and his death was a blow from which they struggled to recover.

Cassidy's daughter, Emmy, remembers Andrew's illness and how deeply his death affected his brothers.

"It was like a chain was broken when he died – they were very closely linked, and his death left a big hole."

While it seems Andrew was the quiet achiever in driving Anangu Tours, there is no doubt that as the more public face of the operation, Reggie and Cassidy both had a significant impact not only on that business but on the success of educative tourism in Uluru-Kata Tjuta National Park and on the gently instructive approach to tourist experiences that continue to this day.

Those who know and worked with the brothers at Anangu Tours and in other endeavours over the years say this is thanks to their instinctive understanding of the need to educate rather than alienate.

The only people who were not Anangu (at Anangu Tours) were some of the interpreters, like me, who weren't Anangu and this wasn't their traditional language, but were lucky that the Anangu decided they could trust us with learning language, which is so important.

Reggie and Cassidy have always been very generous with sharing their knowledge, and with the things they did and do. They have worked in so many different capacities and for different people over the years so they're used to talking to people from all kinds of different places and cultures. They're not as shy as some other Anangu people who haven't had the same level of exposure. They are more used to how different social interactions work.

Because of this they never make you feel conscious of your difference – to them, you're just another person. They are also very keen to pass on knowledge.

Being a woman, I would work with the women all the time but it got to a point where there wasn't always a male interpreter around. Cassidy in particular had the foresight and forethought to understand that the tours still needed to happen but he knew it would be very sensitive to teach a woman about some of the information. Still, he managed to do it and I was lucky enough to be one of the females he taught.

He taught us what we could do and what we couldn't do. Teaching us what we couldn't do was just as important, if not more important, than what we could do. Knowing what we couldn't do in talking about and doing cultural presentations allowed us to explain WHY we couldn't do certain things.

He was very clever. For example, when he was doing a presentation about hunting and demonstrating the use of a spear he would speak in Pitjantjatjara and, as an Anangu man, he would say what he was doing and how the spear was made and I would interpret that word for word, but then he'd say, "You take the women (tourists) over there and you show them about food and the women's things, and I'll take these mob…" And he would take the men. He had enough of a grasp of English to be able to do that.

Cassidy always handled every question (from tourists) with grace; he never made anyone feel stupid, no matter the question. He and Reggie both had a very good grasp of why it was important for people to understand about culture and to try to explain the sacredness. In private conversations with Cassidy, he would often tell me how he really wanted to teach people his family's knowledge. Back when he was a bit younger, he would take people out to his country and spend a couple of days out there to try to get people to understand why it's such special country and knowledge. It's just like what Sammy is doing now with his tours. Cassidy has always understood that Anangu knowledge is sacred and that it's very special. The rest of the world just hasn't figured that out yet – that it's special and that they need to be taught or shown but there's a fine line between educating people and keeping those sacred secrets.

So many people worked with Anangu Tours – many are still in community, but very old now. We had a social club and we'd get together and have social nights. I think we were allowed four cans of beer each and we'd hold these nights at the Anangu Tours depot at Yulara. And we'd sit and have a few laughs and drink our beers.[4]

Another who worked closely with the Uluru family at Anangu Tours is interpreter and archivist Linda Rive[***] who fondly recalls her time with the early operation:

The reason Anangu Tours was established was to provide employment because until then the Anangu rangers had been conducting tours as volunteers. So it was about locals forming their own company and running their own show.

Mayatja is the word for what we would call manager or site manager – the Uluru family are mayatja for that big red rock, so naturally they were the ones who needed to be consulted about activities conducted there.

They were exhilarating days during the set-up of Anangu Tours – I was involved because I'd been working there for some time as an interpreter. I remember Andrew as a ranger but I worked initially with Reggie and Cassidy and Tiku, but I feel particularly close to Cassidy.

I remember him in those days as being young and very sharp. He had a great sense of humour and fun, and I don't think he realised just how funny he could be.

I remember we were conducting training for the Anangu Tours staff because it was thought that if we were going to set up these tours and make them super professional, everyone needed to do a Certificate III in Tourism. We did first aid and what was then called Occupational Health and Safety (OHS) and all kinds of things they might need to know when dealing with and looking after tourists.

Part of that training was looking at how to safely carry sharp things, and we suddenly realised that while, traditionally, men would carry their spears vertically when they were in a large group, precisely for safety reasons, when they were alone it was customary to carry spears horizontally. And that meant Cassidy would have to adjust the way he carried his spears when he was around tourists. He said, "Oh, I'm going to have to carry my spears vertically like a warrior!"

We all laughed, but it illustrated that he was able to recognise and accept that there had to be new ways of doing things if this tour operation was going to work in the modern world.

It was an interesting time because the Anangu Tour guides were going to be working in tourism but they had never been tourists themselves. They didn't know the background of any of the people who were flying in from all over the world and Australia. These tourists would be flying in and staying in a flash hotel in Yulara, and they were coming down and meeting Cassidy as their tour guide. These two vastly different cultures were colliding spectacularly. The Anangu Tour guides had no concept of this, so they had to learn about other cultures, including other Australian Aboriginal cultures.

The fact that they were able to learn all this showed just how much they understood the importance and value of connecting with tourism. Every day their knowledge was growing. To me, Cassidy stands out as the star in all this training in terms of his learning curve. He loved it and really enjoyed it.

And Reggie did well too. All of us formed a lifelong loving friendship because of those days.

Although Anangu Tours is no longer operating, Sammy has taken the baton in helping to educate visitors to his country, drawing on many years of Uluru family contact with tourists to shape his approach.

Sammy:

Paddy was upset to see that people were going into sacred sites, but it was difficult for him to do anything about it (until after they went back to Mimili and then came back again). When they came back again from Mimili the second time, they came back because Paddy wanted to show the rangers where the sacred sites were and the places where tourists shouldn't go.

Mutitjulu had a few buildings when Paddy came back. There was the ranger's quarters (Bill Harney) but there were mostly people camping in tents. The ranger's house was there and there was a workshop as well.

They would come here to sell artefacts to the tourists. They would come from Ernabella, Mimili, Areyonga … all over the place.

Coming here and having contact with tourists has really helped me to come out of myself. When I first came here to Mutitjulu, I was shy and couldn't really talk to people. Then I realised that people wanted to talk to me and learn from me.

They wanted to hear what I had to say and what I could teach them.

Now, I have travelled a lot for different tourism forums and award ceremonies – travelled and met a lot of different people. They all want to say hello and ask where you are from. That's good. People enjoy learning about Anangu. I enjoy learning about other cultures too.

I always say that I went to all these schools when I was a kid but that's not where I learned English and about the outside world, I learned that from tourists, people from all over the world. The people of the world are my teachers.

Sammy's worldliness comes from years of learning alongside his uncles Reggie, Andrew and Cassidy, but also through engagement with tourists. He has a knack, as did his uncles, of soaking up all the information that comes directly and indirectly through tourism and adapting that knowledge to explain things in a way that is culturally comfortable and easily understood by visitors.

Perhaps one of the most striking examples of this ability comes with the analogy he uses to explain why certain aspects of Anangu culture must remain sacred and cannot be shared:

I tell people this: That I am happy to have you come to my house and visit. I welcome you. You can come into my lounge room and look around and I will show you everything in my lounge room. But you can't come into my bedroom. That's my private place.

I learned this from the tourists themselves – how to explain so the tourists would understand. Every day I would have tourists say, "Why is it secret? Why can't you tell us?" They would say that all the time. Every day. These secrets belong to the Anangu but they still ask every day.

I thought about how they would see it and I started to tell them, hey, see this? This is my home. When I come to your home, you say you are happy for me to come to your house. It's yours. I can sit down in your lounge room, but the bedroom is locked and I can't go in there and look around. That's your private place.

I knew they would keep asking and asking unless I could explain it to them so they could understand. And now they understand when I tell them.

When we take tourists there, we tell only some stories. Some others are locked up. It's like when you come to my house. You can come into the lounge room area. You can't come into my bedroom area, you know? Everyone is welcome to my house but you can't come into my bedroom. When I explain that to tourists, they understand.

• • • •

Family lore has it that in 1873, Gosse encountered Paddy Uluru's father during this initial "discovery" of the rock — a meeting that is widely regarded as "first contact" for Anangu with a white man.

**This recollection came from a community elder who is connected and close to the Uluru family but who, through devotion to Tjukurpa and the "proper way" did not wish to be mentioned by name.*

***Linda Rive is an interpreter and translator of the Pitjantjatjara language with many years' experience working with Anangu, including as a Ranger at Uluru Kata Tjuta National Park, and at Anangu Tours in the organisation's early days. Linda is also an oral historian and archive administrator with Ara Irititja, a digital archive for all things Anangu.*

1. From the diary of William Gosse, 1873 – SA Memory, State Library of South Australia.
2. Uluru: An Anangu Story – Don Murray, Film Australia, 1996
3. Uluru-Kata Tjuta Management Plan 2010-2020; Australian Government; Parks Australia 2010
4. Interview at Mutitjulu (October 2017) with Kate Vickers, a ranger with Uluru-Kata Tjuta National Parks who worked with the Uluru family and Anangu Tours. Her insights are reproduced with permission.

I AM ULURU

CHAPTER 13

So Father Uluru Says

White bible, black land,
We've gotta make these people understand,
Prayer and progress go hand in hand,
So Father O'Malley says.

White seeds, black soil,
Open the land and divide the spoils.
Reap what you sow with your own sweat and toil,
So Mother Nature says.

Bring the children to the mission school,
Let us wash away their sin.
If we keep preaching the golden rule,
Maybe something will sink in.

White law, black gold,
That damn Lazarus he won't be told.
He just sits by the gate, talking loud and bold,
So the politician says.

Bring the children to the mission school,
Let us wash away their sin.
If we keep preaching the golden rule,
Maybe something will sink in.

Black bible, white land,
We've gotta make these people understand,
There's no stronger flame than the spirit of man,
So Father Uluru says.

There's no stronger flame than the spirit of man,
So Father Uluru says.

Graeme Connors – 1984

Kindly reproduced with the permission of Graeme Connors and Panama Music Company Pty Ltd.
• • • •

Sammy:

I like country music and I always listened to Graeme Connors' music. I had his albums for a long time. Then I heard this song and I thought, "Hey! He's singing about my tjamu!"

In 2006 I went to Tamworth to the country music festival and I was going to see Jimmy Little. And then everyone said we should go and see Adam Brand so we did and that was where I met up with Graeme Connors. I told him, "Hey, you know that song you wrote about Father Uluru? Well, I am Uluru! I'm Sammy Wilson."

And Graeme Connors was surprised and happy to meet me. He said, "You are Uluru?" and I said, "Uwa. I am Uluru. Paddy Uluru is my tjamu!"

We had a good long talk and he bought me a beer and he said you come and sit down in the front row for this concert. Everyone else was waiting, waiting, waiting, to go into that concert and we just walked through and we sat in the front row.

I really like the song. It's a good song. The words are important. When I hear the words of this song, I think that maybe those Christian people he is talking about, they were carrying that bible but they weren't reading it.

Graeme Connors:

The song wasn't written so much as a biographical work about any particular person as such, it was an observation on the impact of Christianity on traditional Aboriginal culture. I wrote the song in 1984, which was just before the handback and there was a lot of national debate at the time. I did some research and found that, with the best of intentions, Christianity had actually been quite a damaging force within indigenous communities.

At that time, the issue of children being taken from families and placed within mission schools and church-based organisations hadn't exploded into the consciousness of the Stolen Generations, but I think any clear-thinking human being would have arrived at the conclusion that that strategy of removal was not the right way to go about things, to separate children from their families. We all knew it was happening – that children had for decades been taken away and placed in church institutions where they were often mistreated – but it wasn't until fairly recently that it became an issue in the wider public sphere.

My own mother was raised in an orphanage and although she never spoke of being mistreated in a physical sense, there was certainly scarring throughout her whole life, so I had a glimpse of the impact.

In 1984, we were living in Sydney and we had a splendid parish priest at the time who was very socially aware and acutely aware of religion and social justice. He introduced the thought to my head that the largest percentage of Christians in the world are not of European descent. We tend to think of Christianity as a white man's religion and it was an eyeopener for me to realise that something like only twenty per cent of Christians in the world were of European descent.

All these things came together for me in a sense of injustice and at the time, with the discussion about the coming handback of Uluru-Kata Tjuta being so divisive on a national scale, I think I bought into that with the song.

Taking it from the perspective of "white bible, black land" and "Father O'Malley says" that "prayer and progress go hand in hand", that's the old catch-cry that religion over centuries has been about.

The next verse brings it back to the taking of the land – "White seeds, black soil", and it goes on to the more obvious reference to bringing the children to the mission school – "Let us wash away their sin. If we keep preaching the golden rule, maybe something will sink in."

Maybe the golden rule of "do unto others as you would have them do unto you" was completely forgotten in that whole equation of taking children to mission schools.

Looking back at the lyrics now, there's quite a sense of pointing out hypocrisy and I must have been in a fairly passionate mindset at the time.

There was an arrogance about the application of Christianity during that period where, as far as I can see, the basic tenets of

Christianity were completely upended. It was done in a mostly well-intentioned manner because these missionaries genuinely thought they knew best.

I believed strongly as a child in the magic of Christianity and that it was the one true religion, but it's only when you look at the reality from a distance that you get a clearer picture that enables you to be more rational in your thinking.

I felt somewhat vindicated in the writing of this song when it was quoted by Murrandoo Yanner (an indigenous leader from Far North Queensland) during a debate over mining in the state. He mentioned the line "White bible, black land", and I felt then that the people for whom the song had been written had heard it too. The first time I saw Uluru, I felt completely awestruck and then when I went to Kata Tjuta it was then that I really felt the intense spirituality of that country. It's a place of such incredible power and the landscape reached me deeply.

I used the concept of Uluru as "father", but it wasn't ever intended to represent a person – it was more a reflection of leadership to combat the circumstances in which most indigenous people found themselves. The parallel I felt was to have a focus for the energy of the people, and I believe that is the way Uluru and Kata Tjuta is for Anangu. I can only surmise, because what I feel is just a shadow of the deep spirituality these places hold for the families whose country they are.

I didn't perform this song live for a long time. Not only was it very technically difficult to do live because technology wasn't then what it is now, and replicating the unique sounds that introduce and fade out the song was hard, but there had been a bit of a backlash to the song.

I received a letter in the mail, anonymously, with the lyrics printed out and scrawled in red ink was the message "We know what you're up to and it's not going to happen". I was horrified.

Somehow the song just existed as a recording for a long time and it wasn't until the 25th anniversary of my album North, on which So Father Uluru Says was included, that I took the song on the road and performed it live night after night. The audience's reaction was incredible, and I wished we'd been performing it for the past twenty-five years.

Looking back at it now, through forty years of hindsight, I see that it was an inspired song because it was so elemental. It's still as poignant now as it was forty years ago – that's a good thing for me in that I got it right all those years ago, but it's a bad thing in that we shouldn't even be having to discuss (these issues) now.

It touches on everything from the mining boom – "open the land and divide the spoils" – to the nastiness about Aboriginal land rights – "That damn Lazarus, he won't be told" – there were such loud voices saying "What are you talking about, wanting to share the riches with the original inhabitants?". There were so many in the political sphere who just didn't want to hear about it.

Then the song wraps up with "Black bible, white land" – what I was trying to get to was that the true tenets of Christianity are better understood, quite often, by people living simple lives close to the land than those who are finely educated and smartly dressed who come to preach the gospel.

So "Father Uluru" is my embodiment of this mythical leader who sees that the land has been taken and with it the spirit, and the loss on behalf of those people is immense, and the song is pointing out where the fault lies.

It's wonderful and remarkable that we're having the conversation about this song now because it's a song I felt was a gift in many ways.

It came about because in the late '70s, I was still pursuing my career dream, and I started telling my three boys bedtime stories, which somehow got my creative juices flowing. I thought, "I'm going to write an album about experiences in my childhood and things that are happening in Australia now, so my children will have it as a record of my creative life." This is one of those songs.

I love the song. I feel honoured that it's being included in this Uluru family story because I feel it's been a bit of a lost child. I've always incredibly proud of the song, but nobody really noticed it. It wasn't until we took it out on the road in 2014 that I started to get that very powerful positive feedback.

I feel so connected to the Uluru family over this song because I didn't know there was an actual family called Uluru when I wrote it. When I met some of the members of the family, I hoped I hadn't inadvertently offended them by personifying the rock so I'm deeply grateful to find they are proud of it too.

• • • •

CHAPTER 14

"We signed the paper, not the land"

Mutitjulu is the main place at Ayers Rock, and white people have gone through it, having gone around and come from Inintitjara. Having gone around the other side they went through this place. It is a holy cave. Warayuki is holy, it is a truly holy cave.

White girls do not know about this. Black girls do not know about this. This is men's business. It is a holy cave. It is my camp. Uluru is my camp. This is mine, this holy cave.

Yes, this is a holy cave. I alone truly know about this place. I was put into this place. Yes, my fathers and grandfathers entrusted me with this cave. This holy cave. And girls have broken this thing of mine. And I have become very sad. This is my great ceremony, my holy ceremony, my great camp with its holy tree and Mutitjulu on this side is holy. Ayers Rock is holy. I am Uluru and these things are mine. And this is what I have to say to you in Canberra:

A girl has broken that which is mine, my holy cave. And I became very sad. And I am constantly sad. And I am speaking to you. Perhaps you will help me, please. Others have broken my camp, they have gone through it and broken it completely. I don't know, the white people came from afar. I was ignorant of this as a child, but I grew up at Uluru and I became a man, I grew up and became a man and they entrusted me with these places, Warayuki, Uluru. Yes, Uluru and Apara. They are mine. These two places, Uluru and Apara are mine. I became a man there and I learned all about it but I did not teach my sons. Now I want to teach my sons about this place.

Paddy Uluru, Aboriginal Land Rights Commission, submission on behalf of the Central Land Council. (AIATSIS Collection[1])

The man who was and is widely acknowledged, in whitefella terms, as the first "traditional" owner of Uluru and who had begun the journey towards recognition of Anangu ownership, would not live to see this quest fulfilled. Paddy died at Mutitjulu on January 18, 1979. Six and a half years after his mortal remains were laid to rest in the red earth of his ancestors, on October 26, 1985, Uluru and Kata Tjuta and some 132,000 hectares of Anangu land that had become a national park was officially "handed back" to those to whom it had always belonged, and them to it.

Although the fight for recognition had begun much earlier, it was not until the 1970s, after the 1967 national referendum* to recognise Aboriginal people, that the battle gained genuine momentum.

Following the catalytic Wave Hill action in 1966, in which Aboriginal workers at the gargantuan cattle station downed tools and walked off in a bid to secure the right to be paid wages, the ball began to roll in earnest.

In 1971, meetings were held at Ernabella by the then Office of Aboriginal Affairs, at which Anangu – including Reggie and Cassidy and other members of the family – were finally able to speak up about their concerns over the impact of the pastoral, mining and tourism industries on the land, and the desecration of sacred sites.

Reggie and Cassidy were variously involved with land rights actions and organisations and as the sons of Paddy Uluru, their opinions and input were greatly valued and respected.

At the time of handback, Cassidy was Chairman of the Mutitjulu Community Council, and both he and his older brother had been part of many committees, inquiries and meetings throughout the journey to that momentous day, at which they performed inma.

In 1975, the Central Land Council was formed and the following year, the Northern Territory Land Rights Act was proclaimed after the Woodward Royal Commission into the issue handed down its findings.

By the end of that decade, a claim had been lodged for Uluru-Kata Tjuta but although it was agreed by the judge who heard the claim that the Anangu were indeed the traditional owners of those deeply sacred sites, they could not be "given back" because they were part of a national park and could therefore not be subject to a claim.

In that year, 1979, the Anangu were given title to land to the north and east of those sites, but Uluru and Kata Tjuta were not included. They were far too valuable a tourist asset.

That there had even been the suggestion that these uppity blackfellas were trying to get their hands on what was now considered a national icon caused deep and vicious discord in the wider community. Despite some particularly venomous and misguided criticism, the traditional owners continued to try to assure other Australians that visitors to both Uluru and Kata Tjuta would always welcome, but the fight continued back and forth across a terrible divide.

Things came to a sudden head when in 1983, the Hawke Labor government came to power. On November 11 – incidentally a notable date in Australia's history for a number of reasons – Prime Minister Bob Hawke announced that the Aboriginal Land Rights Act would be amended and that Ayers Rock-Mount Olga National Park (as it was then known), specifically including Uluru and Kata Tjuta, was to be handed back to its traditional owners.

> *"This is an historic decision and is a measure of the willingness of the government, on behalf of the Australian people, to recognise the just and legitimate claims of a people who have been dispossessed of their land but who have never lost their spiritual attachment to that land."[2]*

The following day, Queensland's broadsheet, the Courier Mail, carried a headline that made it patently clear not all those Australian people on whose behalf Hawke believed he had acted and spoken agreed: "NT anger on Ayers Rock gift to blacks"[3] it shouted in ominously large black font.

That "NT anger" was expressed most ardently by its then Chief Minister who gave voice to the concerns of tourism operators and the government itself over what they feared would be the loss of a valuable asset:

> *"Ayers Rock is one of the best-known natural features in Australia. It is the (Northern Territory Government's) view that no single group*

should be allowed to dictate who can visit and see this feature. It should be administered in the interests of the entire Territory and Australian communities." [4]

The Prime Minister and the Anangu stuck to their guns and nearly two years later, at a ceremony that to this day remains one of the most important symbolic pinnacles for Aboriginal land rights in Australia, hundreds gathered at Mutitjulu to see Governor General Sir Ninian Stephen hand over the title deeds to Uluru and Kata Tjuta.

With Reggie Uluru by his side, Anangu elder Nipper Winmati solemnly received the framed document to the cheers and tears of the crowd assembled in the shadow of the magnificent rock.

Within minutes, the elders signed a 99-year lease agreement with the Australian Parks and Wildlife Service. In the space of some ten minutes, Uluru and Kata Tjuta again became Aboriginal land under inalienable free hold and was then leased back to the Commonwealth as a national park. A joint management arrangement was proposed to ensure tourists could continue to enjoy the park, and a board of management was established with assurance of an Anangu majority.[5] The first chairman of this board was Uluru family member Yami Lester. The baton has been handed down and now rests in the hands of Paddy's grandson, Tjama Uluru – Sammy Wilson.

The decision was not without deep division in the wider Australian community, with one jarring image from that momentous day of handback showing a plane flying over the ceremony towing a banner that read "Ayers Rock for ALL Australians".

In spite of the discord, the Uluru family has maintained its gentle and dignified approach, leading by example in the quest to educate and include rather than alienate visitors.

I think most Australians understand our love for our land and country. We have belonged to Uluru and Kata Tjuta for thousands of years now and this way we can make sure the place is looked after properly for everyone. **– Cassidy**

Traditional owners Sammy Wilson (Tjama Uluru) with Cassidy Uluru at the sign indicating the western boundary of Uluru-Kata Tjuta National Park, 2018. *Photo: Jen Cowley*

The land was being returned to its original owners, so we were happy. Long ago Anangu were afraid because they were pushed out of their land and because of that, Anangu left. But now a lot of people want to come back. That's good. It's our place. Our land. – **Reggie**

• • • •

For tens of thousands of years Anangu had happily and, mostly, harmoniously lived and travelled across the vast reaches of the central desert regions, at one with the land and Tjukurpa. Within just a few seasons after the arrival of the white man, that balance had irrevocably and swiftly shifted.

Elsewhere in Australia, indigenous history is punctuated by tragic examples of active resistance to the whitefella incursion – referred to by contemporary commentators as the "frontier wars" – but in central Australia there seemed to be less overt opposition to the arrival of the piranpa and the subsequent loss of access to homelands.

To understand this apparent passivity, it is important to appreciate the nuances of Anangu culture, and the mindset and philosophical approach of those who were at the coalface of that swift and far reaching piranpa foray into the central deserts.

Sammy:

The referendum was held in 1967 to recognise Aboriginal people. Before that, no one would listen but after that referendum, people thought, "Oh, these Aboriginal men have something to say". They began to take the Anangu seriously. It took a piece of paper for Anangu to be heard. They started following Paddy around; anthropologists came to learn about the land and the people.

Way back when Anangu met the missionaries and the station people who came in and took the land for cattle, they just showed whitefellas where the waterholes were and showed them the land – because that's what the station people needed to know. So the Anangu just sort of fell into working together with them, because it is the Anangu way to give people the information they need. The Anangu weren't projecting into the future; they couldn't see what was going to happen.

The whitefellas needed the knowledge to survive, the Anangu offered it willingly. Traditionally, and still to this day for many, Anangu take their information from the land which, under Tjukurpa, sets out the proper way of doing things. Anangu are not thinking about what piranpa might call "the big picture". Accepting that thinking comes from the land itself helps to understand how during those days of white colonisation of the APY lands, Anangu so readily offered their precious knowledge of survival without thought for consequence.

There is no word in the languages of this region for "future" or "tomorrow" because the land will tell you what you need to know, when you need to know it. You listen, instead, to what the land and Tjukurpa is telling you for today. That's the only plan you need to survive and that's the way it was for tens of thousands of years.

So the Anangu told the whitefellas what they needed to know and helped them build the fences because that's what was needed. But now, the Anangu couldn't go back because they had already built the fences. Now, looking back you can see what was going to happen; the implications of building those fences. But at the time, they couldn't predict into the future or think about what was going to happen. So once the fences were built, the Anangu would still go and walk their country, but the whitefellas would say, "Hey, what are you doing here? This is my land." And the Anangu didn't understand that the fences they'd put up meant it was no longer their land, according to whitefella way.

For traditional Anangu, there was no future or past, there was just present. They just lived in that day in that time. Reggie Uluru one day asked with amusement why we needed to know all this who, what, when, where, why. He gave his signature chuckle and said, "I'm just here. I'm here now. In this time."

For his generation of Anangu, and those who went before, the only sense of historical story relates to the ancestral or creation beings and Tjukurpa, which is a different concept altogether from the day to day notion of a past. There was no projection into the future as to what might happen as a consequence, so they just simply helped the piranpa build the fences. They had no framework on which to base a forecast of the future ramifications, which were that they could no longer freely walk or hunt that country that had been their homeland since time began.

The fences the Anangu helped to build were more than just physical barricades; they represented social and economic barriers that would last for generations and that still exist today. They couldn't know it at the time, but those fences marked a point in time that Anangu history was forever changed.

Sammy:

It's still a shock to look back and think that this is what happened. That this is our country but because they put fences up it's now their country. Anangu shared their country but (the whitefellas) got greedy. I call it money hungry. That need for money, I think that's a kind of brain damage that started over there somewhere in England. And then they brought that brain damage to here, to our people. It's hard now. They put signs up saying "private property".

It's still happening. The whitefella way is to have a past and a future and they're still trying to force that way on Anangu. "You must think of the future." Saying that's a good thing. Saying, "It's good for you!".

It's about trusting people when they say they are doing the best thing for you. It's about trusting other human beings who you think would have your best interests at heart. So you say "yes" and then you find out that what you've believed was going to be good for you actually is not at all.

Then they say, "Look! You signed the paper". But paper means nothing to us – we live by the land. We signed the paper, not the land. They (Anangu) signed the papers without knowing what they were doing. Then later on down the track, the young people who have the education come along and are trying to point out that those signatures mean nothing because the people who signed their names had no idea what they were doing.

One irrefutable mark of being an owner (in Anangu way) is your birthplace – where you were born. Some of my ancestors were born in Scotland but that's not my place. Can I go back to there and say "Hey, this is my country. I want to say how it's run? Wiya, they would say, "Hey, who's this bloke?"

I wasn't born in hospital, I was born right here across the road there, north of Indulkana, on my country. But now, children are born in hospital not on country. Now when people are born in hospital, they don't have that incontrovertible sense of place.

Even now, there are fences being put up. All these corporations and organisations that are supposed to be for Anangu, but they are still controlled by whitefellas. They say Anangu are controlling them, but the white people are still the boss – like in the station days. Whitefella laws and ways still overshadow Anangu ways.

As the land rights movement gathered momentum and the push towards the handback of Uluru-Kata Tjuta National Park began in earnest, the challenge for the Uluru family and the wider Anangu community was to try to establish, to the satisfaction of authorities, just who the specific traditional owners were. A flood of anthropologists descended, trying to document Tjukurpa and establish family and kinship lines but the well-intentioned quest fell short of the intended mark because they were applying a contemporary western framework to the exercise.

As Sammy points out, traditional ownership "does not go backwards", it follows place to place according to Tjukurpa. The anthropologists unintentionally clouded the issue by applying a whitefella theory of lineage and ownership.

It depended on who was around at the time. Sometimes that was just the best talkers. Anthropologists just listened to who was there at the time. Who did they talk to? Anthropologists made a big mess of it. So, say if I went to Tennant Creek for a visit and I'm just sitting down talking and there's an anthropologist there, he just takes my name down because I'm there and then later down the track I'm (documented) as a TO (traditional owner). Hey, I'm not a TO, I'm just visiting!

The documenting of "traditional owners" without thorough understanding of Anangu kinship, society and, for want of a more accurate description, knowledge ownership and inheritance, has become increasingly problematic.

According to Sammy – who is at the time of writing both the nominal head of the Uluru family and the appointed chairman of the Uluru-Kata Tjuta Board of Management – it is unlikely that anyone included, rightly or wrongly, in the anthropologists' records of traditional owners will want their name removed from that list. Even if according to the proper way of kinship or Tjukurpa they are not "owners" as such, being a documented TO is simply far too valuable a title, Sammy says with obvious sorrow.

> For them it's about money story. It's sad. Some of the more senior people who had senior knowledge weren't there at the time of the anthropologists' visits, so some of them aren't even recognised on the list of TOs. It's like some people and families who live in the city – they weren't born here and they don't live here but they say they are traditional owners.
>
> Me? I was born here – I live here. My kids were born here. I am Uluru.

• • • •

The right for Aboriginal Australians to vote had been granted in 1962, but the constitution did not provide for Aboriginal people to be counted in the census. The 1967 referendum was held to change this and to allow for the government to make specific policies with regard to Aboriginal rights and welfare. The turnout for voting in the referendum was astonishing – some 94 per cent of voters participated and saw the highest "yes" vote ever recorded in a federal referendum with nearly 91 per cent voting in favour of the constitutional change.

1. Journey to Handback – AIATSIS collection, Canberra - aiatsis.gov.au
2. Prime Minister Bob Hawke, quoted in the Launceston Examiner, November 12, 1983
3. Courier Mail, November 12, 1983 (AIATSIS collection)
4. Northern Territory Chief Minister Paul Everingham (AIATSIS collection – Journey to handback)
5. Central Lands Council; Land Rights News Vol2 No1 Nov 1985

CHAPTER 15

"Come, hear us and learn – I AM Uluru"

In a quiet, unassuming corner of the rangers' compound at Uluru-Kata Tjuta National Park, there's a pile of rocks. Little rocks, big rocks. Some the size of marbles, some like fists, some as big as pumpkins. There are black ones and grey ones and white ones. Most are a deep rusty red, the unique signature hue of the astonishing landscape just beyond the headquarters' fence.

Every day, as the mail truck arrives, the mound of rocks grows higher. They arrive in postbags and boxes and envelopes and padded parcels from all over Australia and from every corner of the globe. Some return to this place as anonymously as they left, but most are accompanied on their journey home by apologetic little notes and messages of regret.

They are "sorry rocks".[1] These little pieces of place started trickling in during the late 1970s when cultural awareness began to dawn on the visitors who had souvenired the rocks and now wanted to make amends for their unintended offense by sending the pieces home, to Uluru in particular. After the handback of the park to Nguraritja (traditional owners) in 1985, the flow of returns increased markedly and has continued in a steady stream since.

The growing mountain of sorry rocks poses something of a logistical challenge for the rangers – it's not simply a case of putting the rocks back, so they are catalogued and held along with the letters, to be used when needed to assist in erosion control – but the fact that the messages all express remorse is a measure of the growing understanding that Uluru is not just a rock, not just a tourist destination, not just a tick on a bucket list.

"Kata Tjuta, I didn't even know you existed but you absolutely blew my mind. I sat at a lookout for almost an hour and watched a little bird sail on your thermals. It was a beautiful moment and I took a nearby stone so I could hold a piece of you forever. Uluru, I took one from you too. I wanted to take away some of your magic with me for the rest of my travels, for the rest of my life even. I realise it was wrong to do so, therefore I am sending both pieces back to you. Forgive me for being foolish and thank you for letting me spend time with you and absorb your beauty." (220grams, received January 2014, from France)

Like the pile of sorry rocks, visitor understanding of the sacredness of Uluru has grown and grows still but it wasn't always so.

When this incarnation of the Uluru family story first began with an invitation to spend time with Tjamus Reggie and Cassidy, they and other Nguraritja – under the stewardship of Sammy as the head of the Uluru Kata-Tjuta Board of Management – had been working hard for many years to gently educate the visiting public about the reasons for asking people to appreciate the rock from the ground. However the choice to climb, or not, was still in the hands of tourists.

One bright April morning, I stood with the Tjamus at the base of Uluru looking up along the chain that had long ago been hammered into its ancient spine. We talked about their father Paddy Uluru and their memories of playing around the rock as youngsters and of learning in its shadow the sacred stories of their Tjukurpa. We talked of their time as rangers at the rock, and of the tourists they had met over the years. And we talked about the signs that try to explain to visitors the Anangu plea for them to choose not to climb, signs that are impossible to miss, particularly with two Anangu elders sitting right in front of them. But miss them – or more precisely, ignore them – tourists did.

I watched in awkward embarrassment as one tourist couple went up the chain and another group came down, walking past both the signs and two of the Nguraritja whose requests they bear.

The Tjamus barely raised an eyebrow. They instinctively know that the understanding and acceptance of knowledge comes not

I AM ULURU

at the end of a battering ram, but by immersion and temperate instruction over time. For Anangu, the gaining of knowledge is a lifelong process, the various parts of which add up to an eventual whole, and so has been the traditional owners' approach to the climb. Simply closing the climb to tourists at the time of handback in 1985, as was their right, would have driven an even greater wedge into the divide between Aboriginal and non-Aboriginal, and that would have done neither cause any favours.

As that educational process wound down to its eventual conclusion – the 2017 announcement of the coming closure of the climb – Reggie and Cassidy offered their thoughts for a photographic story book we were working on at the time:

> *"Uluru and Kata Tjuta are deeply sacred for Anangu and have been for a long time. Although they are now popular places for tourists to visit, they have been central to our Tjukurpa for many thousands of years – since the dawn of time. Each marking, each formation, each fold, each cave and view of Uluru and Kata Tjuta has its own significance and meaning for us. This is why we are happy for people to visit and admire these sacred sites, but we worry when visitors want to climb Uluru. It is very dangerous to climb the rock and many visitors have died while climbing Uluru. This makes us very sad. We also worry about the impact of visitors on the fragile environment of Uluru and Kata Tjuta. We ask that people instead choose to acknowledge our traditions and culture by walking around the base of the beautiful rock to learn and discover a deeper understanding of our sacred places. If you are mindful of this significance when you visit, we think you will understand."[2]*

Since then, Tjamus Reggie and Cassidy and Uncle Sammy have shared, as far as Tjukurpa will allow, many stories and insights about Uluru and its contemporary history and do so with a reverence that reflects its ancient history and its place in their sense of identity. This family IS Uluru.

Reggie and Cassidy Uluru with the signs erected at the base of the rock urging visitors to choose not to climb Uluru. The climbing chain was erected in 1966. In 2017 it was announced that the climb would close in 2019. *Photo Jen Cowley 2016*

Cassidy and Reggie Uluru at Mutitjulu Waterhole. *Photo: Jen Cowley, 2016*

Reggie:

My father (Paddy Uluru) said I'm going to take you to see "the range" (the Anangu word for which is arpata) but he meant that he was bringing me to see Uluru.* My father brought Cassidy (who was about seven or eight at the time) and other family members with him. My brother Andrew was still at Mimili. When we got here, we saw that it wasn't really arpata at all – it was a big rock. There is a graded road now, but there were no roads then. We travelled across country. We were walking but we also had a camel. He said it was arpata but when we got here he said, "Here it is. Here's the range." It was Uluru. If he'd told us it was a big rock, we'd have been worried about how we'd climb it so he told us it was a range so that we wouldn't be worried.

Tourists were already here at Uluru then. We saw them when we got here. My father was upset to see tourists going into places they shouldn't be in.

We met the ranger, who wasn't very happy. He said "What are you doing here? This is not your country." And my father said, "No, I AM Uluru. This is my country."

We met up with more brothers and others who were here. A lot of them are gone now but there were other family members here then. I started working as a ranger then.

There are no toilets on top of Uluru, so tourists relieve themselves up there and it all runs down the rock into the waterholes. No swimming in the waterholes now for Anangu.

The warning against the climbing is about safety. We need to spread that message, particularly if people are coming in their cars – they need to look after their tjitji. Because kids these days are crazy. Before the chain was put up, kids were always forbidden to climb. They weren't allowed to climb on the rock, they were warned off. They had to find other places to climb and play because climbing Uluru is dangerous. If they fell, there was no doctor and there might not be a traditional healer around to fix you. It's slippery and you could break your leg. If you break your leg you could be left behind. So that's what they used to say.

I once stood on the base of the rock with Queen Elizabeth when she visited. Somewhere, there's a photograph of me with her. We were standing a little way up the rock, me and the Queen.**

Cassidy:

My father (Paddy) married my mother (Munyi) at Everard Park Station, where Mimili is today. He brought us back to Uluru from there, and there is important story line through all that country for the Uluru family.

This was the first time my father had been back to Uluru since being away and that's when he showed me the rock.

I had no idea what was happening when we came back to Uluru. I was just a kid and I didn't know what to think. I didn't know what the rock was. I was kakulyarani (shocked and awed) and I had my mouth open.

I laugh now because when I first came here, I thought Uluru was a big sand dune!

Sammy:

When he came back to Uluru from Mimili, Paddy was upset to see that people were going into sacred sites, but it was difficult for him to do anything about it. They went back to Mimili for a little bit and then they came back again because Paddy wanted to show the rangers where the sacred sites were and the places where tourists shouldn't go.

Paddy had some help from some whitefellas who had said he should go back to Uluru as soon as possible and tell them (the rangers and tour operators) about which sites tourists shouldn't visit. They helped him because they said otherwise it might be too late.

When they came back to Mutitjulu, Paddy cried when he met up with Joseph Donald who was the youngest one of the four that had been chased away after Paddy's brother was shot at Uluru.

Mutitjulu had a few buildings when the family came back. There were the ranger's quarters (for Bill Harney) but there were mostly people camping in tents. The ranger's house was there and there was a workshop as well.

The climb up Uluru's ribs was made more comfortable and accessible for tourists by the installment of a chain hammered into the rock along the traditional route taken by the ancestral Mala (hare-wallaby men) when they arrived at Uluru. This creation story makes that particular facet of the great rock deeply significant for Anangu. Tjukurpa demands that Nguraritja assume the responsibility for the welfare of visitors to their country and this responsibility is taken very seriously by traditional owners. Each time a visitor to their country is injured or killed by a fall from Uluru (as has happened on thirty-six occasions to date), Anangu are profoundly saddened. This "duty of care" under Tjukurpa is the source of great stress for Nguraritja and grief for the loved ones of those who are lost.[3]

Such is the gentle approach of traditional Anangu teaching, though, that rather than close the climb altogether, the Nguraritja chose choice. Educate not dictate. Carrot not stick:

> *"We are creating guided tours for tourists, and teaching Anangu children and young men so they can do this work. We are showing how to do it properly and they are listening to us – "Oh yes, all right"– they say as they get a good understanding of how to present the tours and talks. On the tours, we welcome the visitors who have come from other places and we make them happy." Reggie Uluru – Uluru Kata Tjuta Management Plan 2010, p.81*

> *"There are many sacred places to respect and Anangu have always said "not over there, here is the right way to go". We take (tourists) to appropriate places and tell them appropriate stories, for example talking about Mala stories or maybe go on the Liru Walk to talk with them*

about our traditional law and stories in a proper way." – Kunmanara Goodwin p.84

> *"That's a really important sacred thing that you are climbing… you shouldn't climb. It's not the real thing about this place. And maybe that makes you a bit sad. But anyway, that's what we have to say. We are obliged by Tjukurpa to say. And all the tourists will brighten up and say, "Oh, I see. This is the right way. This is the thing that's right. This is the proper way: no climbing." Kunmanara (name used for someone who has died) p.90*

In November 2017, after nearly three decades of gentle educational efforts and encouraging visitors to choose, based on that education, not to climb Uluru, the time had come. The decision to close the climb on October 26, 2019 – thirty-four years to the day since handback – was taken neither lightly nor on a whim. Plans had long been in place to close the climb once the number of visitors to the park choosing not to ascend Uluru dipped below twenty per cent.

Careful and constant monitoring by the park's management has kept a close eye in recent years on the mood of tourists, measuring the visiting public's appetite for change.

The chain was first erected in 1966 and extended in 1976 when numbers grew significantly and continued to grow as Ayers Rock's tourism facilities and access were expanded and enhanced. In the 1990s, some seventy-four per cent of those who came to visit Uluru did so to climb it. By the time 2015 rolled around, this figure had plummeted, and park figures showed that fewer than twenty per cent of tourists climbed the rock, choosing instead to experience Uluru from its base.

While there remains a pocket of discontent within the wider Australian community over the decision to close the Uluru climb, most people at least accept the significance of the rock to Anangu and are comfortable with the decision. They have come to this understanding and knowledge in the ancient way of Anangu teaching – learning through listening, by attrition and immersion rather than through direct instruction or decree. Wise Anangu, like Reggie and Cassidy, have always understood that it is only through coming together with the other inhabitants of this contemporary world in which we live that the secrets and traditions of an ancient past will be kept safe.

It was in his role as chairman of the Board of Management of Uluru Kata-Tjuta National Park that Uncle Sammy Wilson stepped up to the media's microphones on October 31, 2017 to announce the coming closure of the climb. But it was as Tjama Uluru – grandson of Paddy Uluru, nephew to Reggie and Cassidy Uluru, father, grandfather, uncle to the next generation of an ancient family line and keeper of an ageless flame – that he carried such an historically and culturally meaningful message to the world:

> Anangu have always held this place of law. Other people have found it hard to understand what this means; they can't see it. But for Anangu it is indisputable. So this climb issue has been widely discussed, including by many who have long since passed away. More recently people have come together to focus on it again and it was decided to take it to a broader group of Anangu. They declared it should be closed. This is a sacred place restricted by law.
>
> It's not just at board meetings that we discussed this but it's been talked about over many a camp fire, out hunting, waiting for the kangaroo to cook; they've always talked about it. The climb is a men's sacred area. The men have closed it. It has cultural significance that includes certain restrictions and so this is as much as we can say. If you ask, you know they can't tell you, except to say it has been closed for cultural reasons.
>
> What does this mean? You know it can be hard to understand – what is cultural law? Which one are you talking about? It exists; both historically and today. Tjukurpa includes everything: the trees; grasses; landforms; hills; rocks and all.
>
> You have to think in these terms to understand that country has meaning that needs to be respected. If you walk

around here you will learn this and understand. If you climb you won't be able to. What are you learning? This is why Tjukurpa exists. We can't control everything you do but if you walk around here you will start to understand us.

Some people, in tourism and government for example, might have been saying we need to keep it open but it's not their law that lies in this land. It is an extremely important place, not a playground or theme park like Disneyland. We want you to come, hear us and learn. We've been thinking about this for a very long time.

We work on the principle of mutual obligation, of working together, but this requires understanding and acceptance of the climb closure because of the sacred nature of this place. If I travel to another country and there is a sacred site, an area of restricted access, I don't enter or climb it, I respect it. It is the same here for Anangu. We welcome tourists here. We are not stopping tourism, just this activity.

On tour with us tourists talk about it. They often ask why people are still climbing and I always reply, "things might change...". They ask, "Why don't they close it?" I feel for them and usually say that change is coming. Some people come wanting to climb and perhaps do so before coming on tour with us. They then wish they hadn't and want to know why it hasn't already been closed. But it's about teaching people to understand and come to their own realisation about it. We're always having these conversations with tourists.

And now that the majority of people have come to understand us, if you don't mind, we will close it.

Visitors needn't be worrying there will be nothing for them with the climb closed because there is so much else besides that in the culture here. It's not just inside the park and if we have the right support to take tourists outside it will benefit everyone. People might say there is no one living on the homelands but they hold good potential for tourists. We want support from the government to hear what we need and help us. We have a lot to offer in this country. There are so many other smaller places that still have cultural significance that we can share publicly. So instead of tourists feeling disappointed in what they can do here they can experience the homelands with Anangu and really enjoy the fact that they learnt so much more about culture.

Whitefellas see the land in economic terms where Anangu see it as Tjukurpa. If the Tjukurpa is gone so is everything. We want to hold on to our culture. If we don't it could disappear completely in another 50 or 100 years. We have to be strong to avoid this. The government needs to respect what we are saying about our culture in the same way it expects us to abide by its laws. It doesn't work with money. Money is transient, it comes and goes like the wind. In Anangu culture Tjukurpa is everlasting.

Years ago, Anangu went to work on the stations. They were working for station managers who wanted to mark the boundaries of their properties at a time when Anangu were living in the bush. Anangu were the ones who built the fences as boundaries to accord with whitefella law, to protect animal stock. It was Anangu labour that created the very thing that excluded them from their own land. This was impossible to fathom for us! Why have we built these fences that lock us out? I was the one that did it! I built a fence for that person who doesn't want anything to do with me and now I'm on the outside. This is just one example of our situation today. You might also think of it in terms of what would happen if I started making and selling Coca Cola here without a license. The Coca Cola company would probably not allow it and I'd have to close it in order to avoid being taken to court. This is something similar for Anangu.

A long time ago they brought one of the boulders from the Devil's Marbles to Alice Springs. From the time they brought it down Anangu kept trying to tell people it shouldn't have been brought here. They talked about it for so long that many people had passed away in the meantime before their concerns were understood and it was returned. People had finally understood the Anangu perspective.

That's the same as here. We've talked about it for so long and now we're able to close the climb. It's about protection through combining two systems, the government and Anangu. Anangu have a governing system but the whitefella government has been acting in a way that breaches our laws. Please don't break our law; we need to be united and respect both.

Over the years Anangu have felt a sense of intimidation, as if someone is holding a gun to our heads to keep (the climb) open. Please don't hold us to ransom. This decision is for both Anangu and non-Anangu together to feel proud about; to realise, of course it's the right thing to close the "playground".

The land has law and culture. We welcome tourists here. Closing the climb is not something to feel upset about but a cause for celebration.

Let's come together. Let's close it together.[4]

• • • •

* *Paddy brought his sons Reggie and Cassidy, along with other family members, back to Uluru in around 1958/59, returning to his spiritual home for the first time in more than twenty years since he fled in 1934 after the shooting of his brother. They travelled on foot and by camel, with Paddy taking his sons on an educational journey following a series of waterholes along the family's storyline from Mimili to Uluru – a distance of more than 300km.*

** *Despite our best efforts we were unable to locate a photograph of Reggie Uluru with Queen Elizabeth, and while there is no reason to doubt his recollection, some family members believe it may have been Princess Diana whom Reggie met and was photographed with. Both Reggie and Cassidy have met many visiting dignitaries over the years, including the Dalai Lama during a 2015 tour of Australia and have done inma (traditional dance) on many occasions including for various royals.*

1. Uluru Kata-Tjuta National Park fact sheet; Parks Australia, 2015. Note: The park authorities are now trying to downplay the role and notion of "sorry rocks" for fear the practice implies that Anangu have somehow cursed the rocks.

2. Anangu Wai (Hello People): J.Cowley, 2016 – Kungka Kutjara Aboriginal Corporation

3. Uluru-Kata Tjuta Management Plan 2010-2020; Australian Government; Parks Australia 2010

4. Statement by Sammy Wilson, Chair of the board of management of Uluru Kata Tjuta National park, executive member of the Central Lands Council and Director of Uluru Family Tours – Central Lands Council, 2017

CHAPTER 16

What's your name, son?

"What's your name, son?"

The lad looks down at the knot of his long brown hands, clenched on the desk in front of him.

He's been dreading the question. He's been fearing the question for most of his ten years, bracing himself against the humiliation of a roll call in each new classroom.

In the jigsaw puzzle of a school-yard world, where he just wants to fit, where he longs for the security of sameness, he is different. He is a foreigner. In his own country.

In a world of Brendans and Billys and Bretts, he is Tjiangu.

He knows what's coming. The teacher will stumble over the word, each attempt falling awkwardly from a twisted tongue.

"T...ch...jang...tach..."

And his classmates will giggle, every titter a painful little barb in his youthful bravado.

With his caramel skin, thick dark hair and deep obsidian eyes, Tjiangu's ethnicity is a guessing game for grown-ups.

"Is he Afghan? Mediterranean? Eastern European? But his name...he doesn't LOOK Aboriginal."

He's not white enough to be white. Not black enough to be black. He's apakatja – half-caste.

At a tender ten years old, he's already balancing on a tightrope of identity. As the years pass, as the boy becomes the man, the ravine on either side of the divide will deepen. The stakes will climb higher. He will grow into his name and to all it means in his quest to know who he is, where he is from, where he belongs. It will lead him to his country and guide him to his identity. When asked, he will offer it with pride.

Right now, with his head bowed, his fingers knitted in a tense little bridge and the new teacher waiting for his response, he wishes he was a wog. There's a mob of wogs at this school. But there are no blackfellas.

He's the only one with a name like Tjiangu. It's an oversized coat he can't shrug off. It swallows him up, hiding all that he is beneath it. They don't see him. They see the name.

Tjiangu.

He hates it. And part of him hates the part of his father that gave him the name. He knows he shouldn't. He knows the name comes with roots that reach deep down into the red earth of his heritage and in time, those roots will be the warm embrace of belonging for a young man at the vanguard of a new generation of proud Anangu.

But at ten, the roots feel more like chains.

The substitute teacher is growing impatient.

"What's your name, son?"

Tjiangu looks up, his intense black eyes locking with the man's.

"It's Barry, sir. Barry."

• • • •

Tjiangu (TJ) Thomas is conscious of being just one of many who call Sammy Wilson "Uncle" and Cassidy and Reggie Uluru "Tjamu". His connection is more cultural than direct kinship, but he is accepted as part of the Uluru family through immersion in its embrace.

Tjiangu's great-grandfather (in piranpa way) was a prominent ngangkari throughout the Pitjantjatjara lands and his father, Andrew, is an Anangu man who went through ceremony at Docker River (Kaltukatjara) where his younger son was conceived. Tjiangu's name was placed once the infant returned to community and it is this name that brought him back, as a teenager, to his country and to the people he calls family.

There are others of his generation who are, he knows, more closely placed in the Uluru family story but it is perhaps his place on the peripheral branches of the family tree that makes him well able to articulate his insights.*

I am Tjiangu Thomas. I came back here to Uluru when I was around 17. I was conceived here. This is my country. My father is Andrew Thomas and he went through ceremony here. We are Anangu.

It was my name that brought me back. I was always interested in my Aboriginal heritage, so when I finished school, I came here and started working as an interpreter for Anangu Tours. I learned my language (Pitjantjatjara/Yangkutatjara) from Tjamu Reggie and Tjamu Cassidy and Uncle Sammy. I understand the language a lot more than I can speak.

They were the golden years when there were businesses running and there were lots of positive things happening in community. I think that was a lot to do with great communication – the government invested a lot in helping people to learn Pit, which gave the people the opportunity to really immerse themselves in their language and culture and have a bi-lingual and bi-cultural environment. It wasn't perfect, but there were lots of good things about community then.

Cassidy and Reggie reminded me a lot of me and my brother Rameth, and also Uncle Sammy and his brother Harry Wilson. This is a special place for brothers here at Uluru. In our Tjukurpa there are examples of two brothers, for instance in the Seven Sisters creation story. That was what I think gave me a special connection to Reggie and Cassidy, through that narrative of brothers and brotherly relationships. It's a similar thing with Sammy and Harry – they are brothers but they are so different. Sammy is an action man, while Harry is more of a critical thinker or a philosopher. That's very similar to my brother Rameth and me.

I was accepted immediately as part of the family – I was told, "This is your place, your country". My connection was strong right from the start. I was only still quite young so I didn't recognise this time as the point of connection. It's only really through hindsight that you identify these pinnacle points in your life.

Growing up with my name, I hated my father in a way. I was always picked on and singled out and made fun of because of it. That's why I really related to Uncle Sammy and his struggle with his name when he was young – he didn't want to be called Tjama Uluru, he wanted to be called Sammy Wilson. That resonated so deeply with me.

For one whole year I went through primary school calling myself Barry. I had a mate whose father worked on a building site and when they didn't know what a bloke's name was, they'd just say, "Hey Barry" – sort of a joke. We started doing it at school for a laugh. Then we had a substitute teacher and I just decided to tell him my name was Barry – it lasted for a whole year, until teacher/parent night. The teacher was talking to my mother and father about their son Barry, and they were going, "Who's Barry?" I got a hiding about that.

As I got older I became more and more grateful for my name because it made me realise you can't escape who you are. I have a deep connection to this place – this is my country. I belong here. My name gave me that sense of where I belong.

I'm proud of my name now but back then, as a kid, it was embarrassing. I went to a school that was pretty white – there weren't any Aboriginal kids. I had to change my language – the way I spoke – and so many of the things I was used to doing. Spending time as a young kid in country towns like Alice Springs, Port Augusta, Yalata, Kununurra, then moving to the city, you can't go 'round just chasing kangaroos and lizards, or swimming in the waterholes and rivers and finding animals. You can't do that in the city. I had to change the way I spoke too.

But doing all those things as a little kid – being out in the bush - gives you a good grounding in culture. You're amongst animals, for instance, so when you hear a story about a particular animal you think, "Oh, that's why it acts like that, or that's why it moves like that or does that."

I went from being a straight-As geeky kid to not applying myself at school when I went to Adelaide. I think it was just the urban environment and the sorts of kids I was mixing with who didn't have that grounding I'd had. Again, I didn't see it that way then but now when I look back, I think it was just that absence of cultural reference.

I was grateful for the opportunity to come here but at the same time, I was in a way embarrassed because when I came here I knew so little about my country and my culture. That made me upset with my father in a way, for not teaching me all these things when everyone else had been taught a lot of things ethically and morally – things that were linked to my culture. My parents instilled strong values, but not about being comfortable in my own skin and about my identity. I was struggling to identify myself.

To go from communities in the country where everyone is really black to the city where everyone was really white, I didn't know where I fitted in – I looked more like Afghan, or Mediterranean or Greek. I didn't really feel Aboriginal.

I'd meet girls, for instance and when I'd say, "No, I'm actually Aboriginal" they'd walk away or they'd say, "Oh, I've never met an Aboriginal who dressed like you" – that sort of endemic racism.

The word "apakatja" means half-caste. That's what I've been told I am my whole life – by blackfellas and whitefellas. I'm apakatja – half caste.

That's why sometimes it's so hard for half-caste fellas to find their identity. There are a lot of fellas who feel they're neither one nor the other; that they don't belong anywhere. That's not a racial thing necessarily. Everyone at times is going to feel like they don't belong. But if you have a welcoming community, that helps you to feel you have a place in this world.

When I got back here to Mutitjulu, the family really embraced me. The older men taught me so much (Reggie,

Cassidy, Sammy, Harry). They were really kind – they would defend me when people were laughing at me for how much I didn't know. They would say, "He's okay – he's still learning."

I think Uncle Sammy said it the best. He told me "Life is like a highway for you – you're going to have white lines and street signs telling you where to go and what to do. But you always stick your tyres to the black road. You need to stay within the white lines but you still have your wheels on the black road, and you can go off road too – onto the dirt road."

I took that to heart. I took it to mean that there are choices in life. I'll always have my culture and I will always have my Aboriginality, but I also need to live in the modern world and take the opportunities presented by it.

Uncle Sammy told me, "You have a lot of potential in terms of business and knowledge. It's all good to have great knowledge of culture, but you also need to know people – you need to have a balance." What I learned from Uncle Sammy is that I need to have those white lines as well to know how to operate in the world, especially from a cultural point of view. I think a lot of people struggle with that.

I have very warm feelings when I think of Reggie and Cassidy, but they're also tinged with sadness.

I think of Cassidy – to go from the wonderful, kind person I knew through working with him and staying with him and learning from him, to now see a man go through so many emotional changes – to see all the bad things and how straddling those two worlds hasn't worked in many ways. There has been so much loss. It's been difficult to watch him descend into feeling powerless – I think it's the same for Reggie too, and a lot of elders.

At the same time, there are lots of warm and funny memories too – sitting around the campfire and telling stories. Reggie has held onto his inner child – he has an innate happiness. He finds joy in the little things now and he's always laughing. I wonder sometimes how he can be so joyful when there's so much sadness and bad things happening, but he manages to see the fun in things. He's always joking and playing pranks with the young fellas and making us laugh.

Cassidy is and was much more of a thinker – for me, he was a great mentor. He wouldn't say a lot, but he taught me so much. It's hard to articulate. You'd be sitting by the fire just relaxing and talking about nothing in particular, then he'd just hit you with a truth-bomb and it would shake you and wake you up.

At times his words would just shatter me, but in a positive way. I thought I knew how things operate and work, and then Cassidy would come up with some intense truth and I'd be forced to redesign my thinking. That was really good for me because I found myself being forced to re-evaluate and see things in different ways.

Harry was the same. They wouldn't say, "You're wrong" but they would say things like, "Why do you think that's happening?" or "Why do you think they're doing this or that?" and I'd say, "Dunno, don't care" and they'd say "You have to care". They forced me to look deeper and understand. Forced me to care.

Anangu teaching isn't sitting down getting instruction as such. The passing on of knowledge is like a process of attrition. You learn by just sitting around talking and listening. It's not like I'm specifically looking to learn something or they sit you down and say, "Right – today we're going to learn about…" It's more learning by immersion. You just sit and listen and you'll think, "Oh, that's something I don't know" and you listen more.

In his later years, my lesson from Tjamu Reggie has been to hang onto that inner child and remain joyful and look for the happiness in the little things.

From Cassidy, I've learned to know what is sacred and hold onto things that are sacred. For instance, his relationship with his wife who he still talks to every night, even though she died some years back. That kind of special relationship is sacred – something to aspire to and to be valued.

From Uncle Sammy, I've learned the value of being strong – not just physically, but verbally and emotionally – and to never be ashamed of who you are. He's taught me to always stay true to and be who you are. He saw that I was struggling to find out who I was and where I would end up and he helped me to overcome that.

From Harry, I learned how to think. To be more enquiring. He helped me to see that there's a circular thing happening. There's a circle operating at the bottom with a little bit of knowledge about what's happening up in the top circle. Harry and Sammy are up here in the top circle, so when they tell you something, you take it on board and you store that knowledge even though you don't know exactly what's going on or why you need to know it. You just trust that they are giving you this knowledge for a reason and one day you'll understand. If they say it's going to be okay, you trust them because they have that knowledge and they are up there in that top circle.

That struggle to straddle both worlds is real. I'm not sure I'll ever really get the balance right. When I was growing up, I wasn't black enough and I wasn't white enough. I wasn't cultural enough. I wasn't this enough or that enough. And with my name, always being questioned about it, in a funny way helped me to know who I am. I was always having to think about it because I was always being questioned about it. Once you know who you are, you're a lot better off because you know that connection.

I did have a lot of resentment when I was growing up because of my name but now I really appreciate it. In a way it toughened me up. I'll always have that connection through my name. Knowing that my name links me forever to my country gives me the sense of where I belong. Being a half-caste has been difficult, particularly because I had the conflict of being one half Aboriginal – among the most oppressed people in the world – and half British, among the greatest oppressors in the world. You're kind of at war with yourself. But then I think I've been very lucky to have both my mum and my dad being such strong people. They guided me in the right direction.

I've travelled overseas quite a bit and that opened my eyes so much. I realised at a young age that the media and society help perpetuate the negative stereotype of Aboriginal people. It doesn't matter what good things are happening in a community, it's the bad things the media focusses on. It can be easy, as an angry young man, to buy into that stereotype and see yourself only as oppressed but when I travelled, especially to a place like Peru, I realised there are many other people in the world with similar struggles. The Aboriginal people of Australia are not special in that way. We're special, but we're not the only ones. I went to Peru on an educational exchange and when I got there I realised, "Hey – these people are just like us." It's the same all over the world for indigenous people. It was really eye opening.

Being exposed to alternative history was a huge eye-opener. I wondered how come all this isn't part of the narrative of our education. When you're taught about indigenous studies in Australia, there's only one view presented. I remember watching a video at school once and it was in language and I understood the language but the subtitles were different. I said, "That's not what they said" and I got in trouble for questioning it, even though I was the Pitjantjatjara speaker. At school once, I was literally rapped over the knuckles for calling Ayers Rock "Uluru".

So it's been really interesting that the narrative has changed so much from what actually happened. I wasn't wrong in my thinking, but I was told I was wrong and if you're told often enough you start believing it. I get so angry with the media perpetuating the stereotype of Aboriginal society and disadvantage because it becomes a case of self-identification for a lot of young fellas, a self-fulfilling prophecy.

Travelling has given me the opportunity to see different historical perspectives and to therefore consider the different perspective of indigenous history here in Australia.

Our educational narrative has only really told half the story, at least that's how it was when I was at school. They didn't teach the story of the stolen generation or of the massacres or any of that. People look at that history and say, "Get over it" but in the next breath say "Lest we forget" on Anzac Day, and say we should never forget that. But they've just told Aboriginal people to "get over it".

Whole populations were wiped out, and history and culture was lost and knowledge is gone. That's the most painful part for me.

As cheesy as it sounds, the future is about working together. Acknowledging the past but not dwelling on it. Too many people get side-tracked with the debate. The debate is on a narrow field and timeline, particularly when you only have five minutes in the media. They're reducing the narrative of thousands of years of history to a thirty second media grab. That's why so many people in this area are reluctant to engage with the media. With the intervention that was sparked here in Mutitjulu, a lot of people are fearful that that's the context in which history will be viewed because that's the perspective that was presented.

Acknowledging Aboriginal history and the truth is important. Going overseas and seeing other indigenous people's culture being so highly respected and revered, and then coming back and seeing our culture disregarded in so many ways, by tourists in particular who are ignorant to the fact of that alternative narrative, is frustrating.

Travel has definitely made me more compassionate, but weary because I see that so many other cultures and languages around the world are also dying out – just as ours is or will be. I'm glad there is a push to establish archives and to preserve our culture, but there's a difficulty with our culture because it's almost exclusively oral. And then with Tjukurpa, there's so much that just can't be told to the outside world and it's only passed on orally through particular family and kinship lines, so if those lines break down, how do we preserve that knowledge? It's a balancing act because on the one hand, you want people to understand our culture and to value its preservation, but on the other hand you don't want to destroy what's sacred by not observing the sacredness of that knowledge.

Education is the key – to explain to people why things are sacred and why they need to remain sacred, and hope they accept that.

Take, for instance, the climb (of Uluru). There has been a lot of work done to educate people about the reasons Anangu don't want people to climb Uluru and tourists have been given a choice. There's a clear division between people who are disrespectful and climb Uluru, and those who are respectful and choose to learn about the history and the culture.

When I'm doing tours (as a ranger), I often get a lot of negative stuff. I've been sworn at by people who say it's their right to climb. It's really shocking that people will complain to traditional owners about not being able to climb. They'll say, "I've just spent a thousand dollars coming here and now they're saying I can't climb it, that's just bullshit" and then they'll ask you your view! And I'm always like, mate, you're barking up the wrong tree asking a traditional owner. Usually it's the aggressive bloke who just wants people to agree with his view, but most people are respectful.

Education is definitely the right way. Now that it's been decided that the climb will be closed, they won't have a choice but I think it's the right way to have gone to have put so much education into the lead up to closing the climb.

If there's one thing I'd like non-Aboriginal people to know, it's that they need to learn about this country's history, particularly this area, but in general. I don't want non-Aboriginal people to feel any guilt, but they should know about it. I think that would go a long way towards restoring respect for Aboriginal people and would help to address that sub-conscious stereotyping and that cognitive bias.

I would like to see the schools teaching (traditional) language. It's difficult within the framework of the existing curriculum but it's important. Language is key to communication of culture. I would really like to see young people being proud of their culture and to know their language and culture but also know how to operate in both worlds.

People say I do it really well, but I'm not sure I always do. I struggle all the time, but people don't always see that. There are things I think I should know but don't. Sometimes you feel like you're expected to be one or the other – black or white. I've seen that take a terrible toll on young fellas, some who have taken their own lives or turned to drugs or alcohol because they just don't know where they fit.

Giving kids a sense of a sense of identity and place and belonging is vital, and a lot of that can come through language. The first thing the colonists did was to take away language. That took history and knowledge. That's how you supress a culture.

The more I learn and the more I do with Aboriginal culture, the more I want to work towards its preservation. I can see how much hurt the stolen generation has gone through because of the horrible effect of not knowing where you belong. You're visibly Aboriginal but you don't feel it. You don't have any connection so you don't identify.

If I'm lucky enough to have children, I'd like them to know their Aboriginal history and culture. I might even take a leaf out of my dad's book and give them an Anangu name. That's tough, because I know how hard it can be with a blackfella name in a whitefella world. I think of that embarrassment every time they called the roll at school – they'd stumble over my name every time and I'd feel humiliated because I felt different. All the kids would laugh at me. You're supposed to be proud of your name, and I am now, but then it was difficult to see that it was so valuable.

Anangu want a better life, but they're being told what to do and it's not making life better. As a nation, as a whole, people are struggling with identity and it's the same for Anangu. There's negative and positive. It's like a coin in that it has two sides. But in order to see both sides you have to know it has two sides so you can turn it over and over and understand both sides. If you're only looking at one side of the coin, you don't see the other side – you think that's the way things are, but you're not seeing the different perspective.

Everything has changed a lot over the years, but back in the day things were easier. All the little things now tend to get in the way of what's really important – the big things. When you go to countries where people have nothing, you often see that they're happier.

I want to share Anangu culture with the world and in that way, protect it. I feel a responsibility to help carry the flame. I felt it even when I was younger and that led to a bit of conflict with my dad who was worried about me coming back here – I think he was concerned I might take a different, more destructive path – but now he's proud that I've found my place.

This is my place. I am Anangu. I am Tjiangu.

• • • •

* There are many others who belong to the Uluru family whose voices are not represented in this book, but are no less important to the story. Some gave background information but asked not to be named directly; some chose to have others speak on their behalf. The logistics of gathering information and recollections meant it was largely those who were available for interview at Mutitjulu whose input appears. This is in no way a reflection of the depth of kinship for the extended Uluru family.

CHAPTER 17

"We all live under the one sun"

Much like any sweeping generational saga, the Uluru family's story is one of love and loss, of tragedy and triumph, of trial and tribulation. But it is also a collection of ancient and contemporary cultural and social experiences and revelations that, viewed collectively and stitched together with empathy and understanding, weaves an extraordinary tapestry from which we observers, as well as the new and coming Uluru generations, have much to learn and consider.

For while the Uluru story is an ancient one, much of the turbulence that punctuates its retelling has come from recent history and the changes responsible for that tumult have come with often brutal swiftness. The challenge now is, as it has in many ways always been, for Anangu to find a way to adapt to and live with and around those changes.

The family will continue, as will the story but what will be written on those future pages?

Sammy:

I'm working now and it's expensive when you go out bush with the young fellas to teach them because you have to travel and camp with them and that's expensive. I use my own money to do that.

Sometimes the government doesn't see this as important education. They might fund the community but the money is tied up and it doesn't always get out to where it needs to be. They give the money, but they don't give Anangu the job of doing the teaching themselves. We are not asking for a lot of cash for ourselves, we just want some help so we can take the young people out bush for education and training

in traditional things, which includes things like managing and looking after the land.

It's really important to me that the young fellas learn the traditional ways. It's still important. I can see it getting smaller and smaller. People's knowledge is being lost. I can see it happening. I see "Disney way". It's coming – we're going to lose it.

This is our homeland. The country is still ours. It's still the same. But the younger generations' knowledge is getting smaller.

It is really important that we teach and educate our young people with traditional learning. The government doesn't see that this is an important investment in young people because it helps stop them from going wrong way. I wish someone had been a bit tougher with me when I was young.

This is not about finger pointing. This is about community solutions to a community problem.

Reggie:

I would like to do a big painting of all the waterholes, showing where they are – that would be good. People, especially young ones, could look at it and learn and they would say, "This is what Reggie taught us."

I want to be able to take the young people out bush and to show them everything about their country; all the different species and foods; camp out by the different waterholes and soakages. To see and learn about the perentie, the kangaroo… all the different foods and learn all the things like my father taught me.

I want them to experience it and gain the knowledge of their environment like we did in the past, to tell them how we lived in the past and how we speared rabbits and that sort of thing. Especially the young fellas. When they're growing up and they don't want to hang around with their mothers anymore, when it's time for them to step out and into the

Reggie and Cassidy with their father Paddy Uluru's sacred tree, at Paddy's Camp near Mutitjulu in 2017. *Photo: Jen Cowley*

man's world.

At that age, it's a great thing for a young man. They really enjoy doing it and learning all about the country and seeing that this is the way all the generations before them have lived.

I really feel strongly about taking young men out and teaching them and making sure they know about that way of life and that culture.

Out there on their country and hearing that language and those stories that were their grandfathers' stories, that sustains them and sustains their spirit. They carry that knowledge with them as men as they grow older, that experience and that learning they had when they became men. To know that stuff is good for their spirit. It's very good for people's sense of self and well-being.

If they only know how to depend on store bought food and buying cigarettes, that's no good. What is good is to be out in the bush, camping out and learning the ways and hearing the stories and hearing that wangka (language) – that's the way to feel really peaceful and good in yourself.

Nowadays I feel not strong enough and I get pain and I get short of breath, so it's hard for me to do these things myself with the young men. But I just want to know that they're out there doing this and still learning from other men.

When we are all gone, I'd like my grandsons to be talking about how good it was that our grandfathers taught us all these things; that they took us out bush and showed us our country, told us stories and talked to us and taught us the proper ways about the environment, about how to make spears and hunt for food.

I would like them to remember that it was good to go out with their grandfathers and learn all these things. I would like them to talk about how I was always taking them out bush and teaching them. That would be good.

Alan:

I don't know if Tjukurpa is still strong with young ones. Maybe I think their parents, and sometimes their grandmothers even, have thrown away their own culture. Discarded it.

It's all about motorcars, money, houses, playing cards (gambling) – that's what they think about. When the mothers might be asleep, the tjitji (children) go out and get up to mischief.

Did your mum let you run around like a rabbit all through the night? No, I think your mum said to you, "Come on – kunkun time (time to sleep)! You have to go to school in the morning!" Children need to learn in school and later maybe realise they can use that education to help other people and tell them, "Don't worry about money – that's not everything."

Pukulpa, wiya (No good) some of the young ones. They might have a kind of confidence through having money and other things but they're not happy. They are just dependent on government handouts for their livelihoods. They seem a bit lost. They don't have their Tjukurpa.

The government is encouraging and wanting everyone of working age to be working and earning their own living. People of my age, who grew up in the bush without that money, we don't tend to worry about money so much. We grew up without money.

What I say to my grandsons is that you need to listen to what your grandfather tells you – if you don't listen, if you disregard it, you will end up dying. If you go off and do these things, these no good things, bad things will happen and you will end up dead and your parents and grandparents will be sad.

When I was young I was told by my father "You are growing up like this tree here – you gotta grow up and you are going to be older so grow straight and don't go on the wrong track. You listen and follow my teaching. If not, you will end up in disaster."

Grog, marijuana – it's a problem. That's why people can't think properly. They end up fighting and there's domestic violence. And with marijuana, people end up with a lot of mental health issues and they can't think properly.

Because the government rule transcends us all – it's bigger than me – the police act on those laws and just straight away arrest people and take them to gaol.

Instead, we should be really teaching our young people and showing them right way. Then there wouldn't be so much trouble and families would be well. Parents would be teaching children right way.

We all live under the one sun. There are people who are asleep right now, while we are sitting here in the afternoon sun. They'll be just getting up. Even if you live over on the other side where it's dark there when it's light here – it's still the same sun.

Emmy (Cassidy's daughter):

For our family, the challenge now is to deal with the young fellas who have to live in a whitefella world without the connection to culture. Back in the older days, when we didn't have mobile phones or drugs or alcohol, it was much simpler.

Language is really important but it's hard to keep it because we're living in the modern world with English. The older you get, the more you forget. Until I was six or seven, I was fluent and my language was my first language. I'm starting to get it back but the older you get the harder it is.

I have my own Tjukurpa – I'm Willy Wagtail totem. Growing up around Uluru, you learn the whole thing (as a woman) in a clock-wise direction. That's the general Tjukurpa. Then there's the women's sacred part, and that's something only I know and I will one day pass that on to my daughters. It's the same with men. There is general stuff that we're happy to share with tourists and other people but there is the sacred Tjukurpa that only belongs to the men. Men's business will have to be taught by someone else to my sons. I can't know anything about that. And my boys won't know until the time comes, either.

That's still really important but now we go with the changes. We can't go back to the old ways. We're never going back to living on the land. So we have to move with the times and learn to live in the modern world, but still hang on to our culture. The children must have their education but they also need to know their history and their culture.

It's said the onlooker sees much of the game. Amid the myriad arm's length pontification about the future of Aboriginal communities in Australia, there is a genuine desire to help preserve and maintain the remnants of languages and culture of the oldest surviving indigenous society on the planet. There is a fascination with the Uluru family and its story that draws many a curious observer to the periphery hoping for a glimpse into the family's remarkable world but there are also many who, despite being outside direct Uluru kinship, have a deep love and respect for the family and an empathetic appetite for helping to ensure its survival.

Inherently, both Cassidy and Reggie have kind hearts and they both have a deep understanding that their knowledge needs to be passed on and must not be forgotten. I think that if Cassidy ever reached a point in his existence where that knowledge was forgotten, that would be the very worst thing that could ever happen – it's so important to him.

They both fear a loss of Tjukurpa and knowledge. They have a fear of the impact of the new ways on young fellas, in terms of losing Tjukurpa and knowledge.

They're both very tough men, both very resilient – they've come through some very tough times. But through all those tough times, they've kept their culture and their knowledge, sometimes against incredible odds and that wouldn't have been easy.

The young people today are facing different but no less difficult challenges, and those changes are deeply troubling for Reggie and Cassidy. They fear the knowledge will be swept away by the influence of the big machine that is the dominant (white) culture.

Elsewhere in Australia that loss all happened a long, long time ago but here, it's different. That's the difference when you're talking to Reggie and Cassidy Uluru. When you talk to elders from other places, or regions where that colonisation happened earlier, they're talking about a memory – what's left. Crumbs. When you talk to these men about their culture, you're talking about them becoming men yesterday. It's still very real and still alive. It's not a memory – it's here, don't lose it. Reggie and Cassidy are living icons.

The Anangu inheritance is knowledge – the inheritance is knowing how to survive in this country and knowing how to live the right way. That's how big the inheritance is. It's ensuring that people know the right way to survive in this country.

Those who are living with the present challenges know that the future will not incorporate a lot of that stuff. They know that when those old people are gone, that knowledge will be gone. They know that's happening. They know they're getting chewed up in a welfare, unemployment, illiteracy, substance abuse, family violence crisis situation. They know they have to face those challenges without losing that connection to the past.

The Anangu's is a culture that requires learning events from the day you're born – learning about plants, what flowers when, what happens when it rains, animals, the land – every day of your life. Traditional life required a lot of time to reach the point of being a tjilpi or a pampa (old woman) – how can that be put into a social situation where children are required to attend whitefella school five days a week? They're left with two days a week in which to learn a lifelong, lifetime worth of culture.*

Michael Wilson (Sammy's son):

My name is Michael Apiya (Tjapiya) Wilson. I was born in Alice Springs on December 22, 1993. I was taken straight home to live in Indulkana. When I was a young boy I remember my big brother Ken used to look after me and he taught me a lot. He taught me to ride a motor bike. It was a Pee Wee 50 but the first time I rode it I ended arse up. I still have the scars from when a dog bit me when I was riding it. My dad got rid of that dog quick then.

When I was about five or six my mum and dad sent me to

Oodnadatta to go to school. School was good and I'm happy for what I learned from my auntie and I made a couple of good friends. When I first went there a couple of young fellas fought each other over who would get to be my friend. They ended up both being my best friends as we grew up. But I was lonely for where I'm really from, where I belong.

I remember my teacher told me I had to do a family tree and I didn't know where all my family was or who they were. That made me cry. I always remember that pain. So I came back to my father to learn my bush education; to learn to be a bush professor like him.

It's good to know the animal language, the Tjukurpa stories. To not be lost but be one with my mob, to look after and take care of loved ones.

What's hard is not knowing who my dad's (biological) father was. I always have the question in my mind: what really happened with my grandmother? Did my grandfather ever care about her and us?

I want to show love and respect to my daughter and all my future children. I want them to be good people. I want them to have a happy life, not worrying about money but being strong and free on our land.

I am Uluru. It is my bloodline.

• • • •

Who knows what the next chapters of the Uluru family story will bring?

The Anangu, as with any continuous culture on earth, are destined to evolve and the Uluru family is part of this evolutionary process. Its members understand the inherent challenges of straddling the two worlds – the old and the new; the black and the white; the modern and the traditional – in which they now live. They accept that if their culture and Tjukurpa are to survive, they must adapt. They must somehow find a balance that acknowledges and honours the past, accepts and embraces the present and looks to the future.

Part of finding that balance is to acknowledge the value and wisdom of bringing the outside world along with them on this journey. This book, as Sammy Wilson says, is part of this tentative step:

> It is important for people to understand; to understand Anangu, to understand Tjukurpa. To understand history. This book will be history. If it's read, maybe people will understand. We need to write it all down. We can work together. Otherwise there's a big wall in between us – I can't come across and you can't come across.

The family seeks neither to assign blame nor apportion guilt. They ask simply for understanding through education and the opportunity to return the gesture through their own efforts to adapt and learn.

It is their hope – as it is mine, as their invited storyteller – that readers will consider the Uluru family story in this light and thus help with the preservation and maintenance of this precious culture in a fast-changing world.

They wish for this so that coming generations will have the confidence and comfort of a sense of belonging that comes from an ancient, undimmed cultural flame.

To be able to say, as did their forebears...

"I am Uluru".

• • • •

Kate Vickers is a ranger with Uluru-Kata Tjuta National Parks who worked with the Uluru family and Anangu Tours. Her insights are reproduced with permission

CHAPTER 18

Where I Belong

WHERE I BELONG

By Carnett Brumby-Churchill
(2018 – aged 14)

Tjina nikitina ngaranyi
Manta nyanga nyangangka
Marangka tjukurpa witira kaninyi.
Tjanpi wiyangka
Tjina boot kutju, kampa kutjarangka ngaranyi.
Kalaya ngampuna marangka kanyini
Pakara ankuntjaku, paapakantja wiya
Ngura nyanga nyangangka.
Paluru tjina uti, manta nyangangka
Punu, malu, inuntji wiru
Uwankara kulingka kampanyi.
Nyangangka ngaranyangka, tjukurpa kanyira, kurunpa alarinyi
Ngayulu nguraritja ngura nyanganguru.

I stand barefoot
On this dark soil
Holding life in my hands.
No grassy roots, just
Dusty boot marks on the side.
Unborn kalaya in my hands
Waiting to run but never fly
Across the red, red land.
His footprint on the sand
Trees, kangaroos, bush flowers
Baking like an oven in the outback.
Standing here, holding life, my soul shines
Because this is where I belong.

As the grandson of Sammy Wilson (Tjama Uluru), Carnett Brumby-Churchill is helping to write the next chapters of the Uluru family story. Like so many Anangu of his generation, and like his uncles and grandfather before him, Carnett straddles two distinct but now intricately and inextricably linked worlds. At the time of writing, he is completing his formal education as an Indigenous Scholarship student at The Scots College in Sydney. The connection with his Scottish ancestry (his Tjamu Sammy's biological father was of Scottish descent) is a nice but peripheral consideration in this educational landscape.

Where once, the immersion of a young person like Carnett in the scholastic and social construct of a place like The Scots College would have been at the expense of his Anangu heritage, Carnett is himself the teacher in many ways. Where once he would have been the object of paternalistic assimilation he is now, like his grandfather Sammy, helping to teach an eager new cohort of young fellow Australians about the beauty and importance of his ancient culture.

His poetry signifies a connection to country that remains robust in a world where it could so easily be lost. For all the trappings of a prestigious formal mainstream education, Carnett holds fast to his deep Anangu roots. He will learn both ways and perhaps he too will struggle as do many young men, both Anangu and piranpa, but he has an important sense of belonging to help guide him.

He is the grandson of Tjama Uluru. The young uncle of Cassidy and Reggie Uluru.

There is no Anangu word for great-great-grandfather, so with the perfection of an ancient circular tradition so often played out throughout the Uluru family story so far, Carnett is brother of Paddy Uluru.

He is Uluru.

• • • •

A MESSAGE FROM SAMMY WILSON (TJAMA ULURU)

To young Anangu people, I say this: if you want to know where you belong, if you are worrying about your future, if you are concerned about having money in this piranpa world, then come here to your country. Come and work with and for your family and your people and for your culture and your tradition before it is lost.

We are educating people in the ways of our culture. We are teaching people about Anangu history so we can earn a living but at the same time so we can maintain our culture and preserve our language and heritage before it is gone.

Come join us. Work with us. Remember your sense of belonging.

To non-Anangu I say this: Our culture, our Anangu way, IS sustainable. It has a great contribution to make to the whole of Australia and the world, not just to Anangu. It has a contribution to make both economically and socially, but we must acknowledge the need to invest in the maintenance of culture and language before it is too late. Come with us, learn with us. Let us show you and teach you. Let's work together.

Palya.

GLOSSARY

—

As the languages of the APY/NPY lands were traditionally oral in nature, there remains some variance in the spelling of different words. The spelling of the words contained in this glossary represent just one of those many possible variations.

Anangu – literally meaning person, but generally applying to the indigenous groups of the central and western desert of Australia.
Apakatja – half-caste, of mixed-race descent
Arpata – range (geographical feature)
Inma – traditional dance
Irititja – history (literally, of the past)/ ara irititja (story of the past)
Kakulyarani – shocked/in awe
Kapi – water
Kutatji (man/men) – traditional/tribal enforcer or executioner
Kuna – excrement
Kungka – girl or younger woman
Kunkun – sleep
Liru – poisonous snake
Maku – witchetty grub
Malu/malu-wipu – kangaroo/kangaroo tail
Mamu – evil spirit, ghost
Minga – tourists (literally meaning ants, but used to describe tourists)
Minkulpa – native tobacco
Minyma/minyma pampa – older woman/elderly woman
Ngintaka – lizard/goanna
Nguraritja – traditional owners (literally of this place)
Palya – all good, fine, suitable. This word has become widely used by Anangu and piranpa alike as a universal greeting (okay, hello, goodbye, thankyou) because there are no specific terms of greeting in Anangu languages.
Pika (n.) – pain/illness; pika (adj.) – fight
Piranpa – white (literally, but has come to mean white people)
Piti/coolamon – an all-purpose wooden bowl or carrying vessel
Pukulpa – good, all is well
Rama-rama – mad/insane
Tjanpi – spinifex
Tjamu – grandfather
Tjilpi – old man, wise old man
Tjitji – child
Tjukurpa – Anangu faith, dreaming, law, ways
Unta – daughter (short for untalpa)
Uwa – yes
Wangka – talk (wangkara-wangkapai – talking)
Wati – initiated man
Wiltja – shelter
Wiya – no

ACKNOWLEDGEMENTS

The process of stitching together all the pieces of the magnificent patchwork that is the Uluru family story has not been without its difficulties. Had I known just how professionally and personally challenging an undertaking this project would be, I may have politely declined the family's initial invitation. I'm so glad I didn't. I'm happy I didn't know then what I know now. I'm equally conscious of the fact that if this project has taught me anything about this remarkable family and Anangu culture, it's that the more I learn the more I will never know. And I'm happy with that.

However, I am only the storyteller – there are many people and organisations that have helped to bring the story to life and without them, this project would have been infinitely more difficult if not impossible.

Firstly, I offer a personal thank you to Steve Cowley who is not only a talented photographer, but a patient and supportive husband who keeps the home-fires burning while I chase rainbows. Occasionally, he gets to come along for the ride and I'm so glad this was one of those occasions.

Secondly, to project co-ordinator and all-round Mr Fixit, Mark Horton, who kept the project (and me) on track but also stepped up to the plate as researcher, note-taker, driver, chief cook and bottlewasher, tyre-changer, bush mechanic and snake remover. Mark's ability to stride smoothly and effectively back and forth between the worlds of Red Centre dust and the halls of government and bureaucracy is beyond compare and it is thanks in no small part to his vision that this project was able to take shape. He is a colleague, a mentor and a dear friend.

Mark and I would like to offer our deepest, sincerest gratitude to our remarkable interpreter and cultural conduit, Kathy "kt" Tozer, without whom there is literally no way the retelling of the Uluru family's story could have been possible in this format. Her empathy and understanding, her grasp of the nuances of both languages

(English and Anangu) combined with her ability to straddle what would have otherwise been an overwhelming cultural divide, enabled us all to come together to overcome barriers and forge a respectful understanding. Without kt, this book you're holding would simply not exist and we can't thank her enough.

There are many others to whom we offer heartfelt thanks:

Linda Rive – archive administrator with digital resource Ara Irititja – who generously shared her wealth of knowledge on all things Anangu, assisting with cultural guidance and allowing unfettered access to the remarkable digital archive of which she is one of the architects. She also offered linguistic and contextual suggestions and some recollections of her own with which to enrich the Uluru family's story. Linda has impeccable instincts and a passionate heart for her work, and we are grateful for her support and friendship.

Steve Baldwin, Visitor and Tourism Services Manager at Uluru-Kata Tjuta National Park and his staff: From the outset, Steve's boundless enthusiasm was as swift and genuine for the project as it is with his approach to the Anangu and to the landscape and history with which he is entrusted as park manager. He offered invaluable advice and generously assisted wherever and whenever possible in many ways, including helping to smooth our access to and from Uluru-Kata Tjuta National Park. The man is a treasure.

Kate Vickers, a former ranger and early prodigy of the Uluru brothers at Anangu tours, who offered her observations and insights from a place of deep love and respect and whose input helped enrich both the content and context of the story.

The Mutitjulu Respite Centre management and staff who gave us not only the space we needed with which to spend time with Tjamu Reggie but assisted with our many "field trips". They offered endless cups of tea and impressed us with their gentle and respectful regard for the elderly Anangu in their care. Nothing was too much trouble, no matter the hour.

To Clive Scollay and Tracey Guest, of Maruku Arts and CLC (Central Lands Council) respectively whose understanding of and empathy for the community and the Anangu with whom they live and work is an inspiration. We are grateful for their generosity in sharing their experience and knowledge… and their household goods on many occasions!

The Commonwealth Department of Communications and the Arts which not only funded the project but showed remarkable flexibility in keeping with the unusual nature of the exercise and the consequent fluidity of timelines. Thanks also to many others behind the scenes, such as Kristyn Oxenbridge, who assisted with administrative support.

To the members of Mutitjulu community who have not only tolerated our comings and goings over the years, but embraced us and made us feel at home in their community – we say a heartfelt "palya".

Lastly but arguably most importantly, our deepest respect and thanks to Reggie, Cassidy, Sammy and the members of the extended Uluru family, who trusted us with their stories, enriched our lives and minds with their teachings and touched our hearts with their resilience and generosity of spirit.

We will feel forever bound, with love, to you all.

Palya.

—

Jen Cowley

Based in central west NSW, Jen Cowley is a journalist, editor and author of a number of books including two previous publications on behalf of communities in the APY lands. Her twin passions of community development and storytelling have taken her across Australia and the world in pursuit of a greater understanding and empathy between people of different cultures.

Author Jen Cowley with Cassidy and Reggie Uluru at Mutitjulu Waterhole, Uluru – 2014
Photo: Mark Horton

Jen Cowley and Mark Horton at Mutitjulu in 2014. Cassidy Uluru took this photo

ABOUT THE PROJECT COORDINATOR: MARK HORTON

Also based in central west NSW, Mark Horton works in community development, particularly in multicultural social enterprise and social development both in Australia and internationally. Mark is also an accomplished and award-winning visual artist. This book is the third Anangu-based publication for which he has been project co-ordinator.